Magical Writing
in Salasaca

WESTVIEW CASE STUDIES IN ANTHROPOLOGY
Series Editor: Edward F. Fischer,
Vanderbilt University

Tecpán Guatemala: A Modern Maya Town in Global and Local Context,
Edward F. Fischer (Vanderbilt University) and
Carol Hendrickson (Marlboro College)

Daughters of Tunis: Women, Family, and Networks in a Muslim City,
Paula Holmes-Eber (University of Washington)

Fulbe Voices: Marriage, Islam, and Medicine in Northern Cameroon,
Helen A. Regis (Louisiana State University)

The Lao: Gender, Power, and Livelihood,
Carol Ireson-Doolittle (Willamette University) and
Geraldine Moreno-Black (University of Oregon)

Magical Writing in Salasaca: Literacy and Power in Highland Ecuador,
Peter Wogan (Willamette University)

FORTHCOMING

From Mukogodo to Maasai: Ethnicity and Cultural Change in Kenya,
Lee J. Cronk (Rutgers University)

Namoluk Beyond the Reef: The Transformation of a Micronesian Community,
Mac Marshall (University of Iowa)

Magical Writing in Salasaca

Literacy and Power in Highland Ecuador

PETER WOGAN

Westview
PRESS

A Member of the Perseus Books Group

Copyright © 2004 by Westview Press, A Member of the Perseus Books Group

Published in the United States of America by Westview Press, 5500 Central Avenue, Boulder, Colorado 80301–2877, and in the United Kingdom by Westview Press, 12 Hid's Copse Road, Cumnor Hill, Oxford OX2 9JJ.

Find us on the world wide web at www.westviewpress.com

Westview Press books are available at special discounts for bulk purchases in the United States by corporations, institutions, and other organizations. For more information, please contact the Special Markets Department at the Perseus Books Group, 11 Cambridge Center, Cambridge, MA 02142, or call (617) 252-5298, (800) 255-1514 or email special.markets@perseusbooks.com.

Library of Congress Cataloging-in-Publication Data

Wogan, Peter.
    Magical writing in Salasaca : literacy and power in highland Ecuador / Peter Wogan.
        p.   cm.
    Includes bibliographical references and index.
    ISBN-10 0-8133-4152-3 (hardcover : alk. paper)
    ISBN-13 978-0-8133-4152-1 (hardcover : alk. paper)
    ISBN-10 0-8133-4151-5 (pbk. : alk. paper)
    ISBN-13 978-0-8133-4151-4 (pbk. : alk. paper)
    1. Quenchua Indians—Ecuador—Salasaca—Social conditions.   2. Literacy—Social aspects—Ecuador.   3. Indian magic—Ecuador—Salasaca.   4. Ecuador—Ethnic relations.   5. Salasaca (Ecuador)—Social conditions.   I. Title
F2230.2.K4W64 2003
302.2'244'0986615—dc21

                                                                                    2003006402

Set in 11.25-point Minion

FOR MARIA

Contents

Series Editor
Preface

Actions speak louder than words. Don't just talk the talk, walk the walk. It doesn't matter what she says, it is what she does. In such popular adages, we tend to privilege deeds over words, action over language. But words and language motivate our actions—just look at the intent of the phrases above—and give meaning to what we do. We discount the power and importance of words at our own peril.

Anthropologists have long noted that oral traditions are much more fluid than literate ones—as myths, legends, histories, and stories are passed down through word of mouth, they change, at least slightly, with each new telling. While such an observation may seem obvious, its implications are profound and far reaching. The written word does not prevent successive reinterpretations, yet it binds them in crucial respects. This is to say, writing solidifies thought in a singular fashion. Film and video now serve a similar function, but they have not acquired the patina of permanence that accompanies the written word. A video of a wedding ceremony may be a nice keepsake, but the insurance company will still want to see the written certificate.

All writing seeks to exercise power, either by mandate (for example, laws, threats) or more subtle coercion (which often appeals to notions of common sense, logic, and rationality). Along with literacy emerge language specialists and amateurs, from tribal scribes to internet bloggers, who try to exercise varying sorts of influence and power through the written word. Over the last decades, we have come to better appreciate the power of knowledge, both in the so-called real world (witness the rise of a "knowledge economy") and in the realm of social theory (from the works of Gramsci and Foucault forward). As much of the knowledge we have of the external world comes to us through language, it follows that knowledge-as-power is embodied in and exercised through linguistic channels, of which writing is the most prestigious and institutionalized form. While such a realization forces us to question strict material determinism, we must also take care not to dismiss the importance of material conditions lest we reduce exploitation to nothing more than word games.

This engaging ethnographic study of the Salasacas of highland Ecuador points us toward another magical quality of writing: through nothing more than the written word (and a few photographic illustrations), Wogan is able to virtually transport us to this community of 12,000 Quichua (and Spanish) speakers, conveying a nuanced feeling for everyday life there that encompasses the heavy burdens as well as the little joys. Moreover, he illuminates theoretical concerns of broad import (particularly the nexus of language and power) and connects them to our own society (for example, in comparisons with our own fetishized forms of writing such as driver's licenses).

Wogan begins his narrative with a story of discovering his name written in a witch's book, sentencing him to die a gruesome death. He was told that he could avoid this fate by paying the book's keeper $200 to erase his name. It would be easy to write this off as an Andean form of an ubiquitous religious huckster scheme, and Wogan makes clear that Salasacas maintain a healthy skepticism toward such apparent extortion. Yet, the genius of this work is with showing that this is only part of the story: the "witch" is actually San Gonzalo, a Catholic saint important in the local folk tradition; San Gonzalo's carved image is housed in a nearby town and its caretakers are Spanish-speaking whites (the ethnic Other of Salasaca nativeness); and it is widely believed that individuals supplicate San Gonzalo, along with cash payments, to kill their enemies. It turns out that Salasacas treat San Gonzalo with as much respect and fear as skepticism and resentment. The saint is thus shown to provide a projection screen and a social channel for salient cultural concerns with equality and envy, power and social identity.

Wogan goes on to show how Christianity, a colonial legacy, and current bureaucracies have played into the development of a tradition of magical literacy in Salasaca. He relates a story about "God's book," glimpsed by a friend of a friend whose "near death" experience took him through a hell-like place and on to Heaven, where God checked his book and pronounced him not yet slated to die. Again, it would be easy to write this off as an apocryphal story inspired by religious fervor. But Wogan relates the story's themes (as well as the custom of writing lists of deceased relatives to be read during Day of the Dead ceremonies) to issues of state control, techniques of surveillance and documentation, and the nexus of power and literacy.

This is an accessible, engaging, and theoretically nuanced ethnography. Wogan is able to weave theory and narrative description together seamlessly in a way that builds on the tradition of Andean studies while speaking to anthropology more broadly. In this regard, he makes an important contribution to the Westview Case Studies in Anthropology series and to the discipline as a whole. This series presents works that recognize the peoples we study as active agents enmeshed in global as well as local systems of politics, economics, and cultural flows. Wogan accomplishes this not only through historical and political contextualization but also through clever analogies that relate seemingly exotic Salasacan practices to our own taken for granted behaviors.

In presenting rich humanistic and social scientific data borne of the dialectic engagement of fieldwork, this volume, along with the other books in the series, moves toward realizing the full pedagogical potential of anthropology: imparting to the reader an empathetic understanding of alternative ways of viewing and acting in the world as well as a solid basis for critical thought regarding the historically contingent nature of our own cultural knowledge.

EDWARD F. FISCHER
Vanderbilt University

Acknowledgments

Like the Salasacas and others involved in long-term, personal gift exchanges, I believe the best form of thanks is not to say much, but to do plenty in return. I hope to do the latter for the many people who helped me write this book, but for now I also want to express my deep gratitude to them.

The basic conceptualization of the book is particularly indebted to several scholars. Joanne Rappaport, through her publications on Andean literacy, critical comments on my writing, and guidance since my fieldwork began, has fundamentally influenced this work. Richard Parmentier and Judith Irvine also greatly influenced it by initially getting me to recognize the importance of literacy symbolism and ideologies, and by always keeping major theoretical implications on the agenda of our discussions. More recently, James Howe, Linda Smith Belote, and the anonymous reviewers generously read a full draft of the manuscript with great care and insight. To all these people, I am deeply grateful.

Others have also provided incisive comments on individual chapters or aspects of this work, including Rachel Corr, Norman Whitten, Jr., Benson Salet, Wendy Weiss, Thomas Abercrombie, Peter Waskosky, William Mitchell, Constance Sutton, Antonio Lauria, and Kathryn Earle. When I think of the way these people have shared their knowledge, verbally and in print, I can understand why a Latin Americanist dedicated her recent book to all researchers in her field; without such guides and interlocutors, we would be at a loss. I certainly feel indebted to these colleagues, and this feeling extends to all those who have commented on preliminary thoughts that I have presented at conferences and in classrooms during roughly the past decade.

A special word of thanks also goes to my *compadre* David Sutton, who is living proof that humor is vital to the anthropological imagination. David read every page of this manuscript, sometimes in several iterations, and he always offered succinct, telling criticisms. It is hard for me to imagine anthropology without David. It is also hard to express my gratitude to him, but he knows that someday, and that day may never come, he can call upon me. . . .

Ted Fischer, Karl Yambert, and Norman MacAfee also improved the manuscript with their expert editorial advice and sharp insights into anthropological writing, and I greatly appreciate their support. Also, my mother, my father, and my close friend Keith Scribner, three professional writers with distinct talents, pored over individual chapters and helped me steer clear of bad writing habits; if exceptions remain, it is only because none of them could get through to me. Their encouragement was certainly always inspiring.

Various institutions and programs generously provided support, including an Andrew Mellon Fellowship (1990–1994), a Dissertation Year Fellowship, Brandeis University (1996–1997), a Jane's Travel Grant for Latin American Studies (Summer 1997), a Junior Faculty Research Leave, Willamette University (Fall 2001), and an Atkinson Grant, Willamette University (Summer 2002). My colleagues in Ecuador at FLACSO and here at Willamette University, particularly Pam Moro and Rebecca Dobkins, also provided a supportive, stimulating environment within which to bring this project to completion.

I am grateful as well to the directors of UNIS in Salasaca for granting me permission to research and write about their culture, and to the many Salasacas who generously shared their lives with me. I am particularly indebted to Alonso Pilla, who, as I explain later, expertly guided me through his culture. Alonso, *manchanai agradecish nini. Canda mana cungarishachu huanuñgama.* I am also lucky to have been able to use many of Dennis Pippen's excellent photographs of Salasaca.

Finally, I especially want to thank my wife, Maria, without whom none of this would have been possible. From the fieldwork in Salasaca to the discussions about which photographs to include here, Maria has been my partner, my soul mate—*mi vida.*

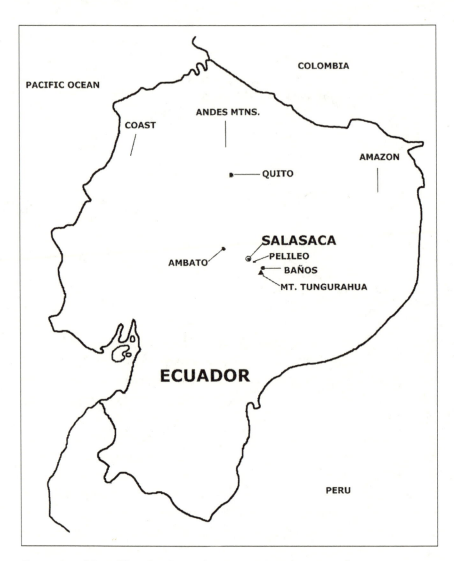

Figure 1.1   Map of Ecuador. Drawn by Maria McIvor (not to scale).

1

Introduction

OVERVIEW

While carrying out fieldwork in highland Ecuador, I kept hearing about a witch who killed people if their names appeared in his book. Then one day in 1995 I was stunned to find my own name in the witch's book—sentenced to die with blood dripping from my nose and ears. I was equally stunned to hear the woman who managed the witch's book say I would be spared if I paid the equivalent of $200 to have my name removed. After asking for clarification, I finally offered the woman a small fee for my visit to the witch's house and said I'd get the rest of the money from a bank in the city. She accepted my payment, but an argument ensued between her and my companion, Jorge, an indigenous man who, the woman said, still owed her money from a previous visit. With Jorge insisting that he didn't owe anything, the argument grew increasingly heated, until finally the woman's daughter and one of her friends started to pull the wool poncho off Jorge's back, saying they would keep it as collateral until he paid what he owed. The daughter and her friend acted at first as if this were all in the realm of good-natured persuasion, but when they got the poncho up over Jorge's head, it became clear they were serious about taking it. Jorge, though, was just as serious about keeping his poncho, his only protection against the cold mountain air and the product of many hours of shearing, weaving, and dyeing. Fortunately, he managed to pull his poncho back down around his shoulders and break away from the others—at which point I realized our visit had definitely come to an end. As Jorge bolted down the street, I followed right behind him, yelling something over my shoulder to our pursuers about coming back to pay them later. After sprinting until we were confident we had escaped, Jorge and I finally stopped, looked at each other, and laughed with a mixture of adrenaline-fueled exhilaration, relief, and trickster's delight at having dodged punishment.

It is not only even easier to laugh about that experience now, from a safe distance, but also to recognize its significance. In this book I interpret such witchcraft beliefs as a serious phenomenon: a sophisticated indigenous commentary on church and state power. Contrary to initial appearances, these beliefs are not the naive responses of a group unfamiliar with literacy; quite the opposite, they reflect almost five centuries of contact by an indigenous Ecuadorian group, the Salasacas, with church and state documents. Beliefs in witches' books and other magical writing crystallize the Salasacas' understanding of the connections between power, social identity, and documentation. It is as if the Salasacas have acted out the scene in *Like Water for Chocolate* where the mother burns her daughter's birth certificate to obliterate her memory: in both cases, official documents ultimately determine individual identity, memory, and existence. The Salasacas have not seen the movie or read the book, but they know about the tomes that contain documents like birth certificates, baptism records, land titles, and tax records. And they have noticed the power of these books, including their power to determine whether someone exists in the eyes of state or church authorities. An Ecuadorian state advertisement proclaimed, "If children are not registered with the state, it's as if they don't exist."[1] The Salasacas have taken such messages to heart and translated them into their own terms, for their own purposes.

Yet, as exotic as beliefs in magical writing may seem, analogous beliefs exist in European/North American societies. Recent research has emphasized the way seemingly mundane state documents can shape the way people view themselves, making groups virtually appear and disappear from the social landscape. Adding a bubble for "Hispanic" on the U.S.

census, for example, introduces a classification, a way of cutting up the social world, that can influence ethnic self-conceptions. A person who never had to think much about such matters may start to confront new terms and identities when filling out forms for financial aid, a loan, or the census. Should Tiger Woods check off African American or Asian on these forms? Moreover, what about the millions of hyphenated Americans who don't have the luxury of transcending such categories by saying "I'm just trying to play golf"? As much as some people might like to dismiss bureaucratic categorization, this is not always a possibility. Since everything from electoral district lines to government funding is determined by state documentation, vociferous public debates about state categories often arise, as in the most recent U.S. census, and these categories, or ones deliberately created as alternatives to them, eventually become incorporated into everyday language and consciousness. Terms like "Hispanic" enter common parlance and affect self-conceptions; census documents, birth certificates, and passports routinely give birth to U.S. "citizens" and other social groups. As one author put it, "The categories used by state agents are not merely means to make their environment legible; they are an authoritative tune to which most of the population must dance" (Scott 1998:82–83).

State documentation is ultimately important to everyone, not only ethnic minorities. When I ask my students every semester which rites of passage move them from the status of youths to adults, students of all backgrounds mention acquiring their first driver's license; as these students recognize, state documentation transforms social identities. You are only known to the state insofar as you have completed such rituals and had your name and information entered in one of its archives. The Ecuadorian government's statement that people who aren't registered essentially don't exist could have just as easily been made by a clerk at the Department of Motor Vehicles after failing to find someone's name in the computer; and the situation is far worse for an entire group permanently left out of the computer databases and paper archives. Like the witch's book, U.S. state documentation can kill.

Unfortunately, previous research has largely focused on state classifications without providing on-the-ground examinations of non-elite groups, especially in non-European/North American societies. *Magical*

Writing aims to fill this gap by providing an ethnographic study of literacy beliefs and practices in Salasaca, where I have carried out field research since the mid-1990s. This book therefore brings two well-established research traditions to bear on each other: political, historical studies of state documentation (e.g., Corrigan and Sayer 1985; Guevara-Gil and Salomon 1994; Kertzer and Arel [eds.] 2002; Scott 1988) and anthropological studies of literacy (e.g., Rappaport 1994a–c; Street 1984).

Yet readers do not need any particular interest in these theories, nor even literacy itself, to benefit from this account. Literacy symbolism serves here as a window into Andean culture, from Day of the Dead and witchcraft rituals to tourism and weaving designs. When I first set out to study Salasaca literacy, I imagined spending many hours in classrooms, *not* running from the owner of a witch's book, yet I came to realize that I could learn as much or more about writing by investigating witchcraft and other ostensibly unrelated phenomena.

Not only did the connections between things like weaving, witchcraft, and literacy eventually become clearer to me, but those connections evolved into the central argument advanced here: beliefs about documentation provide a telling commentary on power, an ideal vantage point for discovering reactions to church and state institutions. Far from a narrow topic, literacy symbolism leads to the heart of power relations—in Salasaca and elsewhere. Indeed, whenever bureaucratic authorities and local peoples interact, archival documents are the central focus of the interaction.

Calculations by development economists illustrate the global magnitude of these issues, as well as their practical implications. Hernando de Soto (2000), for example, points out that the overwhelming majority of people in the developing world and former Communist countries lack legal title to their lands and property, and he calculates the worth of their untitled assets at $9 trillion, twenty times the amount of direct investment pumped into the Third World since the fall of the Berlin Wall. De Soto would like to see ownership of those assets officially recognized, so that marginal groups can use them as collateral for entrepreneurial ventures, but time and again he finds the same obstacles—legal corruption, red tape, byzantine bureaucratic rules. A recent interview ends with de Soto's reaction after reading about South Pacific cargo cults organized around bills of lading and purchase orders: "De Soto loved it. 'They're close!' he said, laughing. 'They just need to get a little more secular'" (Miller 2001:49). This may be true, but de Soto and other development planners also need to get a little more cultural if they don't want their proposals to fail.[2] Moreover, de Soto's calculations demonstrate that millions of people around the world are caught up in a cat-and-mouse game with the state and other bureaucracies. It behooves us, on both practical and theoretical grounds, to investigate these peoples' beliefs about bureaucratic documentation.

On theoretical grounds, beliefs about documentation inevitably take us to the heart of resistance strategies, in particular, yet researchers have been slow to pick up on the importance of such beliefs. It seems resistance studies have been influenced by James Scott's original configuration of this field as the study of the critical, potentially rebellious acts kept away from the direct gaze of official power. Oral expression, in this view, is ideal for resistance because it is decentralized, hard to trace, and open to inflections that vary according to performance contexts (Scott 1990:160). Presumably Scott also steered clear of literacy symbolism because he wanted to concentrate on domination with a strong psychological element—the capricious beatings, the humiliations and indignities that subordinates must endure. Scott states that his "analysis is thus less relevant to forms of *impersonal* domination by say, 'scientific techniques,' bureaucratic rules, or by market forces of supply and demand" (1990:21, note 3).

Yet, even within these original parameters, literacy symbolism is relevant to resistance studies, not only because writing inevitably remains nestled in oral contexts, but because bureaucratic operations regularly involve personal interactions and the sorts of indignities Scott has in mind. Scott would undoubtedly agree, having more recently explored the importance of documentation (Scott 1998); I am simply merging these two aspects of his work, in a non-European/North American context, to gain an expanded sense of resistance and power conceptions.

The Salasacas' ostensibly exotic beliefs also throw into relief the unconscious cultural rules that guide behavior in places like the United States. Reading about Salasaca should ultimately produce the ticklish, uncanny feeling that emerges after reading about the exotic "Nacirema" culture (Miner 1956) and realizing it is actually America (spelled backwards); or experiencing the "estrangement effect" of revolutionary theater, "momentarily shocking us out of 'a general familiarity, of a habit which prevents us from really looking at things'" (Weismantel 2001: 122). When this happens, the Motor Vehicles Department, note taking in class, and other pervasive, taken-for-granted writing practices suddenly start to seem like interesting cultural phenomena. Along with other anthropologists, my goal is to make the strange familiar and the familiar strange.

Starting with the former, in the next section of this chapter I recount several stories about the Salasacas' tensions with neighboring ethnic groups, as well as the challenges of my fieldwork. In Chapter 2, "Witchcraft and Writing," I continue describing my experience with the witch's book, interpreting these witchcraft beliefs as a negative commentary on church and state documentation, with an internal critique of community divisiveness as well.

Chapter 3 reviews Ecuadorian history to identify the specific documentation sources that have most influenced beliefs in the witch's book, as well as the other magical lists considered in later chapters. I argue that these beliefs are most inspired by baptism books, birth certificates, and other documents that track personal identity, and I spell out more explicitly the theoretical importance of this argument.

Chapter 4, "God's Book," examines reports about people who have died, gone to Heaven, and been sent back to earth by God, a male bureaucrat with a book that lists the correct date on which everyone will die. God, unlike the witch, is not amenable to pleas to alter his book, revealing a strict image of power.

During the Day of the Dead (Chapter 5), archival power is appropriated in a way not seen with the other lists: each household uses a list of ancestors' names to imitate archives and honor the dead. Taking stock, I compare all the magical name lists, and argue that these beliefs complement Andean origin myths and devil pacts by adding a window into bureaucratic power.

The penultimate chapter, "Weaving and Writing," turns the gaze more directly on European/North American culture. It shows that, contrary to

European/North American assumptions, Salasacas do *not* compare weaving and writing as mnemonic devices; instead, they compare the two as skills that require concentration and repetition of minute hand movements. I also consider the possibility that my own writing—a weaving pamphlet for tourists and this book—could reproduce power inequalities by defining Salasaca cultural identity.

In Chapter 7, I consider the book's contribution and suggest possibilities for future research.

ETHNIC CONFLICT

Salasacas are essentially considered indigenous because of their ties to the cultures that preceded the arrival of the Spanish conquistadors in the sixteenth century, ties most clearly marked by language and dress. Whereas Ecuadorian "whites" are generally monolingual Spanish speakers, the Salasacas' mother tongue and preferred language is Quichua, a northern version of the Quechua language spoken since the Inca civilization prevailed throughout the Andes Mountains prior to the arrival of the Spanish. Most Salasacas under the age of thirty-five are now bilingual, having learned Spanish through at least several years of formal education and countless hours of television viewing (television first arrived in the 1980s). Yet conversations during a televised soccer game or soap opera still take place in Quichua, just like all other conversations among fellow Salasacas. Even in the presence of whites in nearby cities, Salasacas continue talking Quichua among themselves without embarrassment. Whites can detect a Quichua accent when Salasacas do speak Spanish, but even more noticeable is Salasaca dress, which can literally be spotted a mile away: the men wear black ponchos made from sheep's wool, and the women wear colored shawls, wide belts, and other handwoven items (see Figures 1.2 and 1.3).[3] This traditional clothing clearly identifies the Salasacas as indigenous. Ecuadorian whites, on the other hand, identify more with the European/North American world, especially Spain and the United States. Accordingly, they wear typical European/North American clothing and would be embarrassed to be caught in a poncho or plant-dyed shawl.

Figure 1.2   Baltazar and his son, Jesús, wearing traditional dress for male Salasacas: black poncho, white hat, and red cloth over the shoulder. Baltazar farms, sells tapestries, and plays the violin in a local band; Jesús attends school. (All photos taken by the author unless otherwise noted.)

These ethnic divisions overlap with class and geographic differences as well. Salasacas live in the countryside, whereas whites predominate in the cities (though some live in the countryside as well). Salasaca is located at about 8,000 feet above sea level, nestled between towering snow-capped mountains (see Figures 1.4 and 1.5). On a sunny day, the temperature reaches roughly 60 degrees F, but it drops precipitously at night, sometimes damaging the crops, which consist mainly of corn, potatoes, and grains. The more fundamental problem is the dryness of the land, partly the legacy of colonialism, when the most fertile lands were taken by whites, and partly the result of overpopulation; as a fourteen-square kilometer village of approximately 12,000 people, the land is greatly stressed and cannot support everyone. Many Salasacas therefore complement (or replace) their farming by weaving tapestries for tourists, or working in construction or other jobs in nearby cities, espe-

Figure 1.3 Victoria in traditional dress: white hat, green shawl, beads, black skirt. Victoria and her young daughter also wear a wide, brightly colored belt (chumbi). Behind Victoria is her husband's tapestry loom. Photo by Dennis Pippen.

cially Ambato, the provincial capital, located thirteen kilometers away and accessible by buses that run all day long (see Figure 1.1).

Given all these differences, whites from Ambato and other neighboring cities resent the Salasacas for holding the nation back from allegedly higher, European/North American ideals of progress and civility; the ultimate objection is simply that they are Indians.[4] Yet the Salasacas are not backing down. They have retained aspects of their indigenous culture in the face of centuries of opposition, taking a certain pride in their reputation for fierceness in inter-ethnic conflicts.

Nearby whites, on the other hand, view such fierceness with bitter scorn. I had a chance to learn this when I lived with my wife, Maria, in Ambato in 1994, while making arrangements to move out to Salasaca to

Figure 1.4   Salasaca farms and footpaths, separated by plants with sharp points; Mt. Tungurahua in the background. Photo by Dennis Pippen.

Figure 1.5   Snow-capped Mt. Chimborazo, viewed from Salasaca. Photo by Dennis Pippen.

start my research. Her Hispanic-sounding first name notwithstanding (a tribute to her Italian grandmother), Maria grew up as a monolingual English speaker, and her native English fluency, together with her teaching experience in the United States, helped her land an ESL job at a university in Ambato. Maria was enthusiastic about living in the countryside, so I made arrangements with a Salasaca family to move into one of their rooms, recently vacated by a Peace Corps volunteer, and I walked all over Ambato buying blankets and other necessities for our new home. Shopkeepers and others often asked me what I was doing in Ecuador, and when I said something about living with the Salasacas, the reply was almost invariably a matter-of-fact warning about their violent, backward nature.

I remember, for example, sitting in a tiny Ambato store and being introduced by the shopkeeper to a customer, a middle-aged, well-dressed woman who had just stopped by for a soda. Though this is written in my notes, to this day I have a crystal-clear image in my mind of her reaction when informed that I was going to live in Salasaca: "Be careful! [¡Mucho ojo!], they kill people!" As evidence, she referred to an incident several years earlier in which a Salasaca mob brutally murdered two innocent, teenage boys, just because they were white and passing through Salasaca. I didn't want to disagree, but I mentioned that I had visited Salasaca various times and felt quite safe, and I thought to myself that, like most stories, hers surely had multiple sides. Still, when I was in Ambato, I only heard this one side of the story: the Salasacas are murderers. Over and over, I heard from shopkeepers, acquaintances, and friends the same story about the recent murders, punctuated with a common set of epithets for the Salasacas, ranging from "hostile," "surly," and "closed" to "savages" and "brutes" (bravos, resentidos, cerrados, salvajes, brutos).[5]

After moving to Salasaca, however, I began to hear a very different story—multiple stories, actually, but always with a few underlying themes. According to this version of events, the white boys were killed in the midst of an armed conflict, in which the boys drew knives and a gun after robbing a Salasaca man named Vicente.[6] The boys were the most recent incarnation of a long-standing pattern of white abuse and theft. For years, poor neighboring whites had been stealing land, cattle, and other valuables from the Salasacas, openly insulting the "filthy Indians."

Sometimes whites would simply drive up a dirt path in Salasaca, load sheep and pigs into the back of their pickup truck, and drive off. For subsistence farmers like the Salasacas, such thefts were devastating, yet the police from the nearby white town (no police were regularly stationed in Salasaca itself) never caught or punished anyone, despite repeated complaints and precise identification of the thieves.

Vicente was particularly vulnerable, not only because his house was located near the main highway but because he had experienced a degree of prosperity through his weaving business and relationships with North Americans (see Figure 1.6). For example, a friend from the U.S. gave Vicente a television set, which he passed on to his father. This TV was soon stolen by three white males who pulled up to the father's house in a car, crashed through the door, knocked the old man down, took the television, and sped away, yelling that they would be coming back until the "dirty Indians" had nothing left.

In response to such incidents, a Salasaca patrol was revived after nearly thirty years of dormancy, to raise the alarm should any thieves or

Figure 1.6   Salasaca town center, with folk art stores. The church and central plaza are on the opposite side of the road. Photo by Dennis Pippen.

intruders appear. Nonetheless, Vicente's house was broken into again, and his stereo, phone, and some tapestries and tools were stolen. Two weeks later, Vicente was awakened by the sound of someone trying to break into his house, apparently the same thieves returning to finish off what they had started before. Vicente sounded an alarm on a community loudspeaker next to the church, and various Salasacas came out to confront the thieves. In the course of this violent conflict, one of the thieves brandished a gun and one stabbed a Salasaca man, causing him to bleed profusely and fall unconscious. By the end of the altercation, an enraged Salasaca crowd had beaten the teenage thieves to death, and soon afterward the police arrested Vicente (who was released from jail only several years later after national and international protests on his behalf). When news of the killings was released, whites heaped abuse on the Salasacas: buses would no longer take them to nearby cities, cutting them off from essential marketplace exchanges; Salasacas feared that vendors would put rat poison in their food; and the Salasacas were castigated—from the headlines of the local and national press to the street-corner remarks that I was still hearing years later—as "cannibals," "animals," "brutes," "savages," etc. Salasacas usually have less trouble with whites in Ambato than those from the surrounding countryside, the people geographically, economically, and culturally closest to—and therefore intent on distinguishing themselves from—the Salasacas. Nonetheless, the Salasaca killings of the two white boys, "the innocents" *(los inocentes)*, provoked angry censure from whites throughout the region.

This is a complex case, but it certainly demonstrates that ethnic categories like "white" and indigenous are salient in this part of Ecuador, and that tensions exist between these groups. The real issue, it seems, was not that the Salasacas had killed robbers, but that indigenous people had killed *whites*. I was forced to this conclusion after witnessing the sharp difference in reactions when another killing occurred, this time at the hands of angry whites from a town that borders Salasaca. Newspaper stories in 1995 reported that two men from the Coast robbed, shot, and killed the Korean owner of a jeans-manufacturing business in this town. The landlady then sounded an alarm (at 1:30 A.M.), and neighbors emerged from their houses, formed brigades, and tracked the criminals all night long, finally catching them at about 5 A.M. on the borders of

Salasaca. The robbers were then brought back to the town plaza, beaten, and murdered in front of a large crowd of onlookers.[7]

I could not help noticing the similarity with the Salasacas' own killings a few years earlier: in both cases, two robbers were caught and killed by an angry mob. The key difference was that this time the ones doing the killing were local whites from the very same town that the two murdered boys had come from. And the whites killed two blacks, another ethnic group often considered inferior by Ecuadorian whites (Whitten 1965, 1981). The killings were quite similar, but the ethnic roles had been more or less reversed: this time, whites were the killers and the victims were members of a supposedly inferior ethnic group. There were other differences as well, but I thought this case presented a relatively fair comparison with the Salasaca murders, so I was curious to see how whites in Ambato would react to this news.

After first hearing about the killings from my host family in Salasaca, I canceled my afternoon plans and took the bus into Ambato, bought all the local papers, read them over lunch, picked up my mail at the post office, and headed over to my favorite shop, the same one I had been sitting in almost exactly one year earlier when the woman first warned me about the murderous Salasacas. I sat on my usual wooden stool and talked with the shopkeeper, whom I had continued visiting almost once every two weeks when I came to the city to run errands. I was secretly hoping that he would mention the news himself, but after about an hour, when neither he nor any of the customers did (though many had already read the day's paper), I brought it up myself, pulling the newspapers out of my bag. The shopkeeper did grimace and say this was terrible, but that was the closest response to condemnation I heard all afternoon. This killing seemed to bother people much less than the Salasaca murders, if at all. Many had little reaction and implied that, terrible as it might be, it was business as usual. As one customer put it while shrugging her shoulders, "Well, that's the way it is in the countryside." Some pointed out that such punishments deter other criminals; and while this may be true, I never heard any whites make the same point in defense of the Salasacas (in fact, thefts in Salasaca have virtually ceased since the boys were killed). The only condemnation I heard this time came from one of the political authorities giving an official statement in a newspaper.[8] The news articles themselves contained no strong condemnations of "cannibals" and "savages," as they referred to the Salasacas earlier. To the contrary, headlines and photo captions implied that the crowd's actions were justified: "That's How They Killed the Scoundrels," "The crowd, inflamed by the death of the Korean citizen, took justice into its own hands," and "The furious community . . . said they're tired of the injustice of the law. . . ."[9] Despite the similarities, then, the two killings were treated very differently, reflecting white antipathy toward Salasacas and vice versa.

Let me immediately add some disclaimers. These are unusual situations, not everyday conflicts. I never heard about any other vigilante killings while I was in Ecuador, and I felt safer in Ambato and Salasaca than I have in most U.S. cities. The term Ambateños most often use to describe their city, "tranquil" *(tranquilo)*, is apt in my experience. Even if tensions permeate white-Salasaca interactions in this area, certainly not all whites or Salasacas feel the same way about each other; many interactions are amiable, with attitudes varying according to class, personality, and other factors. And I have to stress that I am not trying to judge anyone. If I were, I would have to start with the shameful history of violence and racism in the United States, and note how hard it is to compare with the Ecuadorian countryside, where police and courts are not always available (see Starn 1999).

Nonetheless, both killings demonstrate a simple point: ethnic tensions exist between Salasacas and their white neighbors. These extreme situations throw underlying attitudes into sharp relief, showing emotions seething below the surface. Theorists have rightly emphasized the hybrid, fluid quality of Latin American ethnicity, but at least in highland Ecuador, ethnic divisions remain a fundamental aspect of the social landscape.

It also makes sense to speak of "whites" in this case since Salasacas do as well.[10] Among themselves, Salasacas refer to virtually all non-indigenous Ecuadorians as *chologuna*, the Quichuaized, plural form of a Spanish term perhaps best translated as "low class, mixed-blood white." The Salasacas refer to themselves, by contrast, as *runaguna, cai ladu runa*, or *Salasaca runa*, i.e., "Indians," "Indians from this area," or "Salasaca Indians." I use the term "whites" here for lack of a better translation and in deference to the Ecuadorians who resent the term *cholo*,[11] the more derogatory term used by the Salasacas. I also primarily use the terms "Salasacas" and "indigenous," rather than "Indian," because "Indian" could sound like a translation of *"indio,"* a derogatory term used by some whites to refer to Salasacas.

Thus, the term "whites" should always be read in quotation marks as a tentative gloss on ethnic complexities. And complexities abound, especially when the other major ingredient, power, is added into the mix in subsequent chapters. For now, suffice it to say that Salasacas and whites have viewed each other as separate groups, often at odds.

FIELDWORK AND FRIENDSHIPS

When I lived in Salasaca from 1994 to 1995, and even during return trips in 1997 and 2002, many Salasacas treated me with reticence—and understandably so, given their previous experiences with outsiders.[12] My greetings on the dirt paths were returned perfunctorily, if at all, and rarely with invitations to further interaction. I had to remind myself that in this small village, where few strangers walk the paths and those who do are often associated with past abuse, striking up conversations with outsiders is not encouraged; this is not the United States, where perfect strangers routinely exchange greetings, jokes, and chats in restaurants, on buses, even in the thirty seconds available before speeding away from the toll booth. As much as I still enjoy joking and chatting (as a North American and an anthropologist devoted to collecting others' stories), I learned to expect little from passing, momentary interactions in Salasaca (see Figure 1.7).

But more disconcerting were the dogs that came charging at me as I walked the Salasaca footpaths. Perhaps others could distinguish between the dogs' bark and bite, but to me their barred teeth and blazing eyes seemed like a clear signal that they preferred biting. I learned to shout and make a mock gesture of stone throwing to make the charging dogs back off and continue their barking at a safe distance. The stone-throwing gesture is common in Salasaca—which was why most dogs readily understood its meaning—yet it felt like I had to feign many more throws than my Salasaca counterparts. And I couldn't help wondering a few times if these vicious animals couldn't have been better restrained by their owners.

Yet I tried not to think about this much, reminding myself not only that dogs provide needed protection in Salasaca, where people leave their homes unattended to work in the fields all day, but, moreover, that

Figure 1.7   Footpath. Photo by Dennis Pippen.

indifferent-to-hostile reactions to outsiders are common in other Andean villages. As an anthropologist from a nearby indigenous village reported, "I had had stones thrown at me in Zumbagua, and more curses hurled at me than I could remember" (Weismantel 2001:13). This anthropologist also visited Salasaca itself in 1982, only to meet with frightened reactions on the paths: "As I walked down footpaths lined with agave plants, little figures occasionally appeared running happily down the path ahead of their mothers, or else dawdling contentedly behind. Suddenly looking up and seeing my strange form, they ran in terror to bury their faces in their mothers' skirts" (Weismantel 2001:9).[13] At least I could take comfort in knowing that, by the mid-1990s, Salasaca children were no longer as inclined to run in terror at the sight of a gringo strolling down the path.

But something much more fundamental prevented me from ever taking these passing interactions too much to heart: they stood in utter contrast with the deeply close friendships that I eventually formed with certain Salasacas. When I think of these friendships, the pathway encounters seem like another world entirely.

I naturally became the closest with the families I lived with, particularly Alonso Pilla and his family. While living with my wife in the Peace Corps volunteer's former home, I came to know Alonso well through many visits, dinners, and joint efforts to promote his weaving trade (discussed in Chapter 6). When my wife returned to the United States at the end of the year, I asked Alonso and his wife, Julia, if I could move in with them. They said yes without hesitation, but the discussion immediately turned to the living arrangements that could accommodate me. Alonso and Julia live with their two children, Holguer and Evelina (ages three and fifteen, respectively), in a modest cement house (see Figure 1.8). The house is the size of the average North American two-car garage, though the Pillas own no transportation other than a bicycle, which Alonso jokingly refers to as "my taxi" while carrying his wife on the handlebars to his or her mother's house (a scene always reminiscent in my mind of *Singin' in the Rain*). The pressing question was, Where would I stay in this small house? I had already said I would like to share meals with them (in return for which I would later give them my furniture, among other gifts), but where would I sleep? Alonso pointed out I also needed a place to store my belongings, especially my computer and notes, since his son, Holguer, would love to get his hands all over them. I thought Alonso was joking, but I later came to understand what he meant about Holguer's devotion to mess making, a realization I was to repeat when my own sons were born a couple years later. Even without yet recognizing the extent of Holguer's endearing mischievousness, I was grateful Alonso had intuited my need for privacy, so I happily agreed when he suggested carving out a room for me by partitioning off the main room, leaving my bed on one side and theirs on the other, separated by two wooden walls that didn't reach the ceiling and a middle room with Alonso's bicycle, assorted metal pipes, clothes, lumber, and a sewing machine.

Although I was standing at my desk as soon as I stepped out of bed and walking out the door as soon as I took another step, my new room felt palatial (see Figure 1.9). I hardly noticed the squeaking noises coming from the other side of the wall bordering my bed, where guinea pigs were raised in a tiny shed wedged between the main sleeping room and the kitchen (in a cultural irony, guinea pigs are an Andean delicacy,

Figure 1.8   Alonso's mother Melchora, Alonso, Holguer, and Julia (left to right). The daughter, Evelina, appears in Figure 1.10. Photo by Dennis Pippen.

eaten during fiestas and other ceremonial occasions). In fact, exhausted from walking around the village and speaking Quichua all day, I slept as soundly in that bed as I've ever slept, maybe even too soundly. At least it was hard for the Pillas to understand how I could sleep as late as seven or eight A.M. One morning, as I stumbled to the latrine behind the house, Holguer blurted out, "Peter, you're a sleepy-head!" *(Pedrito, puñisiquimi gangui!)*, presumably echoing something his sister or parents said earlier. I just laughed "Yes, that's me!" and embraced the characterization, knowing the importance in Salasaca of being able to laugh at oneself.

Jokes were, in fact, a constant part of our interactions. Such joking made living with Alonso and his family a pleasure, but reciprocal, teacher-student exchanges were (and are) the real foundation of our relationship. Alonso and his family have always taken a deep interest in my work, enthusiastically discussing every new piece of the cultural puzzle of Salasaca that I bring home, happy to pick up new knowledge along the way. I am indebted to Alonso, in particular, for expertly guiding me

Figure 1.9   Holguer hanging out in my room.

through his culture. In return, I have promoted sales of his weavings (see Chapter 6), and have tried to teach him and his family something about the culture of the United States as well. Whether I'm describing the trip to the moon or the way Americans (over-)use credit cards, Alonso and his family listen with interest, and our conversations feel like a genuine exchange.

Because of my close relationships with Alonso and others, I feel like I know what anthropologist Catherine Allen meant when she wrote, "I have learned the most (and I think this is true of most fieldworkers) from a few individuals whom I can genuinely call friends and teachers, and who see themselves in this light" (1988:38). And, like Allen, I had "to make an effort to seek out other informants" (ibid.), but fortunately Alonso and Julia never impeded these efforts. To the contrary, they encouraged me to visit all their relatives, as well as friends I had met previously. Such introductions created a snowball effect in my personal relations. Even without a special introduction, Salasacas could locate me on their map of social relations, connecting me with a sector of the village and specific, familiar personalities. It helped, too, that I had become the Pillas' *compadre*: by standing as Godfather to Julia's brother during his confirmation, I made myself even more comprehensible to others in kinship terms.[14] The result was a solid personal network and range of relationships, from the families I regularly visited and shared meals with, to people I sometimes visited, and, at the outer limits, acquaintances.[15] In later chapters I continue describing various relationships, but, even there, I center much of the discussion on Alonso, Julia, and several other close friends. It's not that other Salasacas couldn't be quoted in these cases: I don't introduce anything the "inner circle" said that wasn't confirmed by many others, some of whom are quoted at length in various sections. It is just that, judging by previous studies (Sutton 1991), it will be easier to identify with several clearly defined personalities than a smattering of briefly introduced ones.

What especially helped in creating and extending this network was my fluency in Quichua, acquired through long hours spent staring at grammar charts and re-listening to cassette tapes in which Alonso and another teacher, Rosa María, translated my Spanish sentences into Quichua. Fortunately, my blundering first attempts in rudimentary Quichua were always met with patient encouragement from my Salasaca companions. Only a handful of other foreigners had learned the Salasaca Quichua dialect, including two Bible translators (K. Waskosky 1992; S. Waskosky 1992), a Peace Corps volunteer from the 1960s (Hugh Dufner), and a North American anthropologist who started fieldwork in the 1990s (Corr 2000). Especially for Salasacas who had never met these people, hearing me speak Quichua had a ticklish, novelty effect, provoking bemusement and placing me in an unusual category of outsider. I got a sense of the "Quichua effect" when I realized that the Pillas' pet cat was named after the first foreigner Alonso ever met who spoke Ecuadorian Quichua, anthropologist Frank Salomon (see Figure 1.10). I never had any pets named after me, but Quichua opened doors, facilitated interactions, and changed my position in the community.

Perhaps some of my fieldwork methods also helped promote friendships, or at least they were less of a deterrent than other methods might have been. Even before recognizing the full depth of Salasaca misgivings about writing, I was aware that strains in interethnic relations had made the Salasacas wary of outsiders, and that my own presence in the village

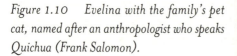

Figure 1.10   Evelina with the family's pet cat, named after an anthropologist who speaks Quichua (Frank Salomon).

could take on a threatening aura, especially since I asked many questions and had stacks of papers in my room. For these reasons, I deliberately avoided surveys, knocking on doors at random, and openly taking notes at public rituals; I made contacts, instead, through personal networks, and wrote notes immediately after observing rituals if I didn't know many of the participants. I also relied on my tape recorder for interviews more than written notes; though both are mnemonic devices, at least the tape recorder doesn't have the same negative associations for Salasacas as written charts and notes. I also rarely took photographs, so as not to interrupt interactions or associate myself with professional photographers, who were rumored to make great sums of money by selling photo books of indigenous people to tourists.

The tourists themselves, who increasingly visited Salasaca to buy tapestries, generally created a positive image of gringos by showing enthusiastic interest in Salasaca culture. Positive images were also established by several Peace Corps volunteers who had worked in the village, organizing agricultural and educational projects. In fact, when I first arrived, I completed a project started by a departing volunteer, painting a world map on the high school wall; and, as noted earlier, my wife,

Maria, and I moved in to the volunteer's former room in a Salasaca home. Adding to the Peace Corps association, not only was Maria teaching English but she also organized games for Salasaca children. It also helped that we were married, since this gave us a more recognizable social identity, perhaps lessening suspicions that could have arisen had I been a single man.

This is not to say that everything was perfectly rosy in Salasaca. Even when I met people through a mutual connection, some were more eager to pursue my friendship than others. Most welcomed me into their homes and offered food and drink, but some directed little conversation my way and didn't mention a specific day when I should come back, signals that were easy enough to read. Although a few strong personalities openly expressed hostility to foreigners, fearing their influence and resenting their imagined profits, none ever bothered me directly. But even the friendliest interactions often began with, and repeatedly returned to, discussions about the price of my hiking boots and plane ticket, highlighting our wealth differences and echoing similar interactions with foreign anthropologists throughout the Andes (Weismantel 2001:186–189). Initially I protested that I was an unemployed student at the time, but for the most part I had to accept that I appeared fabulously wealthy by Salasaca standards. There was no possibility of just blending in, so I continued to wear my hiking boots and customary garb of jeans, T-shirts, and sweatshirts. My strange ways and their initial wariness notwithstanding, the Salasacas received me well for the most part, sometimes extremely well. Curiosity about, if not resentment at, my access to high-priced U.S. goods will probably continue unabated, but by my most recent visit, in 2002, even my boots had become incorporated into a more sentimental view. Alonso and others looked fondly at my boots, and at gifts I had left earlier, as tangible reminders of our shared experiences.

Notes

1. All translations from Spanish quotations and texts are my own. Unless otherwise noted, all translated statements by Salasacas were made in Quichua, and all statements by whites were made in Spanish. Pseudonyms are used, unless otherwise noted. The Pilla family (discussed below) chose not to use pseudonyms.

2. See Hess (1997) for an anthropological discussion of development issues in Ecuador.

3. On the role of Ecuadorian (including Salasaca) dress as a marker of ethnicity, see Belote and Belote (1984); Meisch and Rowe (1998); Miller (1998); and Tolen (1995). On the history and linguistic structure of Quichua (including the Salasaca dialect), see Mannheim (1991); Stark (1985a); Stark and Muysken (1977); K. Waskosky (1992); and P. Waskosky (1992).

4. The terms of belonging are typical of the homogenization process that Norman Whitten, Jr., refers to as "whitening," in which indigenous and black Ecuadorians are admitted into the nation on condition that they surrender their ethnic background, "becoming more urban, more Christian, more civilized; less black, less Indian" (Whitten 1981:15).

5. These epithets were often accompanied by another tale: the one about the Salasacas originally being from Bolivia. According to this view, held by most local whites, since the Salasacas caused so much trouble in their ancestral Bolivia, Inca rulers resettled them in the sixteenth century in their present Ecuadorian location. This is not, however, a uniformly accepted claim among scholars. Although some maintain that the Salasacas came from Bolivia (Rubio Orbe 1965:153; Terán 1972:234), anthropologists Alfredo and Piedad Costales (1959) dispute this idea, historians concur (Nicola 1987[1960]:139; cf. Nicola 1994[1960]:38–40), others point out that the Salasacas could have been relocated precisely for their loyalty and uprightness (Guevara 1945:52), and others remain neutral (Choque Quispe 1992:102), citing a lack of adequate evidence. Since colonial titles linking the Salasacas to Bolivia have never been identified, anyone investigating this issue would also have to consider, in comparative historical perspective, Salasaca violin traditions (cf. Volinsky 1998) and dyeing customs (Masaquisa 1997). What is most relevant here is the way this historical "fact" was presented to me as the quintessential insight that explained the Salasacas' innate belligerence, an obvious attempt to explain the present through the past (Rappaport 1998[1990]; Sutton 1998). As Joseph Casagrande noted, "The reputation of the Salasacas of being very hostile has been maintained by themselves and other people on the basis of numerous legends and stories, repeated many times, about their violence" (1977:88).

6. My account is also indebted to information from several scholars familiar with the case, including one expert who has carried out research for decades in Ecuador, published extensively, and reviewed the lawyers' files and evidence and talked with various parties at that time. I realize that there are multiple perspectives on the killings, with many hotly disputed issues left unresolved, as in most emotionally charged, violent conflicts (Poeschel Rees 2001). For this reason, and given that my goal is only to illustrate the existence of ethnic conflict, I limit my account to the most essential, least-disputed points.

7. This story appeared in *El Heraldo* (July 26, 1995, pp. 1, 10–11A) and the *Extra* (July 26, 1995, pp. 1–2).

8. See "No Killing can be Overlooked," *El Heraldo,* July 26, 1995, p. 11A.

9. These captions are all from the *Extra* article. *El Heraldo* did not offer as much support, but it also did not directly condemn the whites.

10. See Belote and Belote (1984) and Belote L.S. (2002) for interesting discussions of transculturation and inter-ethnic relations among the Saraguros, another highland indigenous group; Stark (1981) on ethnic labels in Ecuador; Whitten (1986) [1974] on Ecuadorian blacks; and Wade (1997) for an overview of scholarship on race and ethnicity in Latin America. For recent arguments on the salience of race in Latin America (and Ecuador, in particular), see Cervone and Rivera (eds.) (1999) and Weismantel (2001). Weismantel also deliberately chooses to use terms like "white" and "Indian," in an effort to make "race more, not less, visible" (2001:xxxiii).

11. *Cholo* can be distinguished from *gringo,* a Caucasian foreigner; see Weiss (1993) on the nuances of this term. *Runaguna* can mean the Salasacas, but it can refer more generally to other indigenous groups, who may also be referred to as "mountain people" (*urcuguna,* i.e., indigenous groups from Chibuleo, Nitón, Santa Rosa), "Otavalan Indians" *(Otavaloguna),* etc. I have occasionally heard Salasacas refer to elite whites (e.g., a rich businessman from the city) as *blanco* or *blanco fino* and non-elite whites as *mishiguna.*

12. My fieldwork, based on participant-observation, took place from July 1994 until November 1995, and July-August 1997, and July 2002. I have also kept abreast of events through regular correspondence with my closest friends in the village, mainly through "cassette tape letters" made with

tape recorders I left, as well as occasional letters and phone calls. At certain points, I will note recent changes as of 2002, but most of what is reported here applies to the 1994–1997 period.

13. Weismantel's examples here form part of her incisive approach to the problem of "fat cutters" in the Andes.

14. See Belote and Belote (1977a) on the dynamics between indigenous Ecuadorian and foreign godparents.

15. I mention meals because they were crucial in creating shared memories and connections. For an excellent discussion of the links between food and memory, with examples from Greece and the U.S., see Sutton (2001). For excellent analyses of food and drink symbolism in Andean contexts, see Abercrombie (1998); Allen (1988); and Weismantel (1988, 1991, 2001:191). Rachel Corr (2002) offers a particularly insightful account of the importance of reciprocal food exchanges in Salasaca itself.

2

Witchcraft and Writing

I now return to the story of the time I found my name in the witch's book. I will argue here that Salasaca witchcraft beliefs constitute a sophisticated commentary on the power of church and state bureaucracies, but to make it clear why this is the case, let me back up a bit, first describing how this witchcraft works and then returning to my encounter with the book.

THE WITCH AND HIS BOOK

The strange thing about this witch is that he's actually a saint: specifically, a Catholic saint by the name of San Gonzalo, the patron saint of the Church of the Medalla Milagrosa in Ambato, the city near Salasaca. As is the case with many patron saints, San Gonzalo is depicted in a life-size statue that stands outside the church (see Figures 2.1 and 2.2). Unlike most other saints, though, San Gonzalo has a rather frightening appearance: he has a sword stabbed into the back of his neck and blood drips from his nose and ears.

According to the church, San Gonzalo is a martyr who died while preaching the Christian faith in Japan during the sixteenth century. A sign next to the statue in the church relates his biography as follows:

27

Figure 2.1   Church statue of San Gonzalo at the moment of his death, with a sword stabbed in his right shoulder and blood dripping from his nose and ears.

Figure 2.2   Shelter around San Gonzalo statue, on the side of the church.

San Gonzalo García belonged to the Franciscan Order, and is considered a mar-
tyr by the Catholic Church. He is Indian, having been born in Bossein, near
Bombay in India. Some believe that his parents were Portuguese. . . . In 1593 the
Governor of Spain sent a delegation of Franciscans [to Japan]. The Emperor
Taikasama accepted them graciously, and they were given permission to preach
in the cities of Mikayo, Nagasaki, and Osaka. Within three years, they had 20,000
Christian converts. But then things changed in 1596, when the Emperor
Combacundoneo ordered the Christian missionaries to leave within six months.
Many obeyed, but others stayed on, disguised, until finally the Emperor
Tagcosano got furious because he thought the missionaries had facilitated the
conquest of Japan by the Portuguese and Spaniards.

The sign goes on to say that San Gonzalo and the other missionaries
were tied to crosses, dropped into holes, cut, and impaled with swords,
and later, in 1862, canonized as saints.[1]

This sort of hagiography, however, is not known or talked about in
the surrounding countryside, where most people—that is, indigenous
groups like the Salasacas and poor white farmers—have a diametrically
opposed view. These people say that San Gonzalo is a "witch-saint"
(brujo-santo)—a saint who has allied himself with the devil, a saint who
uses his powers to harm and kill people. Their conception of the saint is
perfectly logical within the Andean view of the dual nature of supernatural power, according to which good and evil are simply flip sides of
the same coin, like the mountains that can both harm and heal (Bastien
1978; Joralemon and Sharon 1993; Rasnake 1988a).

To get access to San Gonzalo's evil powers, the Salasacas do not visit
the church, but, rather, the house of a private group of whites on the
outskirts of town. These whites, who are in no way affiliated with the
church, actually manage San Gonzalo's books and execute his witchcraft, and they are the ones I visited (and ran away from). The operation
is run by the sisters of a family that could best be characterized as urban,
working-class whites.[2] The sisters access San Gonzalo's power through a
replica of the church's statue, the difference being that the replica is in
their private possession and is much smaller than the church statue,
only about one foot high rather than life-size. The sisters are, in other

words, the caretakers of San Gonzalo, following the traditional Catholic model of saints' "owners" or "sponsors" (*fundadora*, Sp.; *santoyuj*, Q.).

But San Gonzalo's victims are not selected by the saint owners or even by San Gonzalo himself. Instead, the attacks are initiated by poor whites or indigenous people who pay the saint's owners to harm their enemies, with fees ranging from $100 to $200, roughly four to eight months' wages. If possible, the "client" also brings some of the intended victim's personal items, such as clothes, hair, photographs, or dirt where the victim left a footprint. Following a familiar pattern, the witchcraft is carried out through objects that either resemble the victim (the photograph) or objects with which the victim has had close physical contact (the dirt, hair, clothes). In addition, the owners say prayers every Tuesday and Friday night over lit candles, beseeching San Gonzalo to carry out the killing, and eventually the personal objects get burned.

The single most critical method for activating the witchcraft, however, is to have the intended victim's name entered in San Gonzalo's book. The client tells the owners the name of the victim, the owners write that name down in San Gonzalo's book, and the book is placed next to the candles while the prayers are said. On the basis of the written names, San Gonzalo pursues the victim and causes his or her soul to burn up. In most cases, the witchcraft is supposed to result in the victim's death. Sometimes, though, the attack may only cause severe misfortune—for example, turning the victim into a crazy drunkard. But while the hair or candles can be omitted, Salasacas say that the witchcraft would never work without the written name in the book.

Another indication of writing's importance is that the victim can be saved by having his or her name removed from San Gonzalo's book. A victim might first suspect that his or her name is in the book after suffering a sudden misfortune or a persistent illness (the usual signs of witchcraft), or after receiving explicit warnings from an indigenous healer. Based on these suspicions or warnings, the victim goes to the saint's owners and asks them to check San Gonzalo's book. If the victim's name does appear in the book, the victim pays the owners to have the name crossed or cut out, the fee being the same as the amount initially paid by the perpetrator who had the name entered. Once the name is removed from the book (or, in some cases, after the written name is burned, back in the village), the victim is liberated from the witch's spell. In other words, San Gonzalo's book has the power of life and death, demonstrating just how important writing is for this witchcraft.

PERSONAL ENCOUNTER WITH THE WITCH

Many Salasacas volunteered plenty of information about San Gonzalo, helping me piece together a general picture of his witchcraft, but to resolve my lingering, nitty-gritty questions, I always wished for more direct, personal contact with the witch-saint. I wanted to know, for example, exactly what kind of ink was used, what the books looked like, and how they were organized (in alphabetical order? by date?). Despite their ostensible triviality, I believed such details would be the key to pinpointing the specific Salasaca experiences that these witchcraft beliefs reflected and commented on. Understandably, though, these were also the sorts of questions that most people were either unable (due to lack of experience) or unwilling (due to fear of incrimination) to answer. I never pressed the matter because I didn't want to make people uncomfortable and figured that, even if I went to the house, I would never get to see the books anyway.[3] I leapt at the chance, then, when a Salasaca man named Jorge volunteered to take me to see San Gonzalo and even assured me that we would get to see the books.

Jorge is a middle-aged weaver and farmer, bilingual in Spanish and Quichua and literate. He has a boyish charm, reflected in his smile and the twinkle that appears in his eyes, especially when he goes out on a limb with some mischievous or daring comment that takes our discussions to another, deeper level. His boyishness contains no hint of meanness; he often plays good-naturedly with his young sons during or between our interviews, and the same gentle patience infuses his answers to my seemingly endless rounds of questions. Rather than wearing him down, my questions seem to pique his curiosity and analytical inclinations. Perhaps it was for these reasons that one day Jorge announced that, since I was so interested in San Gonzalo, we should just go together to see him in the city. Naturally I said this was a good idea, and agreed to meet him back at his house that coming Sunday afternoon.

Buses constantly run through Salasaca, so on Sunday Jorge and I only had to wait a few minutes by the side of the road before we found ourselves packed into a crowded bus barreling toward the provincial capital. As the bus reached the outskirts of the city, Jorge shouted for the driver to let us off at an intersection. We didn't have to walk far down the side streets of this residential neighborhood before we came upon one of the San Gonzalo owners, sitting on the curb with a group of friends, drinking beer and listening to salsa music blaring from a cheap radio. This woman, one of the sisters who controls the witch-saint, was not exactly intimidating: she was middle-aged, thin to the point of bony, and, when her face lit up on seeing Jorge, her smile revealed missing front teeth. Her tone was also open and friendly as she greeted Jorge in Spanish with the usual series of expressions: "How have you been? Where have you been hiding? It's so great to see you. . . ." The combination of Spanish, salsa, and the look of everyone hanging out on the curb gave the whole scene the feel of a typical working-class, white neighborhood.

And, as in just about any urban neighborhood in Ecuador, this one had a small *víveres* store, with everyday items like cigarettes, matches, candy, soda, and beer. I realized the woman owned this store when she invited us to sit down inside it and called over her teenage daughter to handle the customers that occasionally passed through. Jorge and I sat on a wooden bench in a shallow, dark room bordering the counter, while the woman sat across from us on a rickety metal chair. This wasn't an entirely private setting, but between the blaring radio, the din of the woman's friends carrying on at the doorstep, and the cover from view provided by the wall behind us, it did have a secluded feel, at least enough to allow us to discuss risky topics like witchcraft. Jorge was the one who first raised such matters, asking the woman if she could give us a "look at the candle" *(una vista a la vela, Sp.)*—that is, diagnose our health by inspecting the flames of candles rubbed on our bodies. This type of candle reading is a common diagnostic procedure throughout Ecuador (as well as other parts of Latin America), the white counterpart to the more common indigenous practice of rubbing the patient with a guinea pig and reading the dead guinea pig's entrails for signs of illness.

Agreeing to do the reading, the woman instructed us each to write our names with a pin in the side of a candle, which we then had to rub on ourselves. The owner lit each candle one at a time and stared at the flame, looking for signs that would reveal our physical and spiritual states. After examining my candle, she turned to me and asked if I was married. I said yes, and then she asked if I had had a girlfriend before getting married, to which I again answered yes. She then exclaimed something to the effect of, "Well, that's who's trying to hurt you!" She said my ex-girlfriend was doing this out of jealousy, and that the pain would start in my stomach and legs and eventually spread through my whole body, turning into a grave illness. All of this was news to me and pretty hard to believe, but I decided to play along with everything, putting on a concerned expression and agreeing that my stomach hurt, which was actually true—my stomach did hurt at that moment. Then again, my stomach hurt many other days as well, presumably because of the amoebas that various doctors in the city had detected in my system. The doctors' biomedical diagnosis actually would not have ruled out the possibility of witchcraft; in fact, in retrospect I realize I could have mentioned the doctors' diagnoses as confirmation that I was, indeed, being attacked by my ex-girlfriend (why was I having such a hard time getting better if not because of witchcraft?). Nonetheless, I didn't bring all this up, because I usually tried not to discuss the amoebas with Ecuadorians, and I was still astounded by the news about my witchcraft problem and trying to anticipate what the owner would ask me next. Luckily she didn't ask me many more questions, but just repeated that I had this serious problem, to which I responded with a vague statement about needing to have this taken care of.

Turning to Jorge's candle, she announced that Jorge was also under a witch's attack, one initiated by a neighbor who, after some sort of conflict over land, had hired a witch to pursue him. Jorge asked who the neighbor was, but the woman said she didn't know, so Jorge just accepted the diagnosis, and then asked if we could see the San Gonzalo statue. Agreeing, the woman took the statue out of a cabinet and handed it to Jorge, sitting right next to me. I could see that the statue was quite small, about one foot high, and that it faithfully replicated the church statue's intimidating expression and appearance. I busied myself looking over the statue and listening to Jorge and the owner talk, but, when the conversation started slowing down, I started to feel a bit awkward, with

San Gonzalo now sitting in my lap and staring up at me with that ago-nized expression. (Were we going to say some prayers to San Gonzalo? Was it wrong to keep looking at the statue?) As if to answer my questions about what to do next, Jorge soon handed back the statue, and asked if we could see San Gonzalo's books, since he wanted to see if his name was in there by any chance. Without any expression of surprise, the owner instructed her daughter to go across the street to their house to get the books, and then she herself stepped outside the store for a moment. This pause gave Jorge and me a brief chance to turn to each other and agree in Quichua, a language that presumably none of them understood, that everything was going well, that the woman was quite cooperative.

The daughter came back a moment later with nine books, which we pored over for about the next twenty minutes, ostensibly searching for our names. In actuality, I was just trying to take a mental picture of all the books' particulars—what was written in them, how they were or-ganized, what they looked like, and so on. The first thing I noticed was that, rather than the impressive books I had somehow been expecting, these were just ordinary schoolbooks, the kind that can be purchased for a small sum in any *papelería* or even a *víveres* store like the one we were in. The left side of each page was filled with various names, followed by the words "black mass" *(misa negra)* and prices that ranged from $20 to about $200.[4] My friend noted that the lower prices came from books made several years ago, whereas the higher prices were listed in the newest-looking notebooks. All the writing was done in the same hand, neat and orderly in black ink, and each line had only one name, with a blank line between each name. Some of the name lines had been cut out with a pair of scissors because, as the owner explained, the victim had paid the price listed, the price also paid by the initial client (whose name was not listed). She said cutting the name out of the book was more ef-fective than just crossing it out, since the latter method left open the possibility that someone might still be able to read the name. At one point the owner briefly started to help my friend look for his name, but otherwise she just sat off to the side, answering my occasional questions and even going outside to talk with her friends.

After extensive searching, Jorge and I still couldn't find our names, so we started to give up and get ready to leave. The owner stopped us, though, saying she would bring us one more book to check. This book, which also came from across the street, was much more impressive than the school notebooks: it was a foot high, heavy, and made with sturdy, blue covers and large, lined pages. We searched this book in vain and were about to give up again, but then the daughter asked us for the book so she could look at it herself. Within a few minutes, she pointed to a page where she had found Jorge's name, with a price listed at $160, as well as my own name, priced at $200. As Jorge and I studied our written names with a mixture of shock and skepticism, we were told by the owner that this was a very serious matter, that our lives were in danger, and that we should pay the money right away to get our names removed from the book. She also said that, if we paid, we would get back the personal item left there, which might be sand from a footprint or a piece of clothing. When pressed for more information about the item, she said we probably wouldn't be able to recognize it anyway because we would just get the ashes that remained after it was burned. Stunned by all this, I just said that I would have to go to the bank and return later with the money. As described earlier, an argument over prices ensued, and we then made a hasty exit.

This experience gave me a first-hand understanding of San Gonzalo's witchcraft, confirming and extending what I had heard previously. But other questions remained.

Why Hire San Gonzalo?

The owner's description of my jealous ex-girlfriend and Jorge's angry neighbor was perfectly consistent with the most commonly reported motivations for employing San Gonzalo's services: namely, envy or a personal conflict. For example, another Salasaca man told me that within a short period of time he lost most of his usual tapestry orders, was robbed of a large sum of money while traveling, and was forced to sell off some lands to pay his bills. Although he didn't specify who did this to him, he said somebody must have put his name in San Gonzalo's book because of "envy" *(envidiashca munda)*. "Envy" was also mentioned in stories about interpersonal conflicts, such as the wife who told me that her husband had fallen sick because of witchcraft initiated by his jealous ex-girlfriend, and others who related bitter stories about conflicts with their neighbors over property boundaries. Indeed, "envy" was the most common term used to describe witchcraft motivations, a shorthand for a range of interpersonal conflicts.[5]

Yet, as logical as these witchcraft motivations are, the San Gonzalo's owners' account seemed flawed. I simply could not believe that my ex-girlfriend had come all the way to this little Ecuadorian city to put my name in a witch's book. And it didn't seem like a coincidence that I had first written my name in the candle, and afterward my name appeared in a book stored in a separate place. My guess was that the owners (most likely the daughter) read my name off the candle, wrote it in the book in the other room, and then brought the book to me. This suspicion seemed confirmed by other peculiarities: unlike most other names, no lines were skipped between my name and the surrounding names; the owner's daughter located our names for us; and the price I was supposed to pay was higher than my indigenous friend's. It seemed, in short, like a rip-off operation.

Jorge himself actually expressed similar skepticism once we were safely out of sight and walking back to the bus stop. While I was still debating whether I should reveal my suspicions, Jorge declared that it had all been a trick, that they must have written our names on the spot, that he was sure of this because he did not write his real last name in the candle, yet this false surname showed up in the book. Taking the usual trickster's delight in having subverted a dominant power, he laughingly said they were just trying to rip us off, but that we had been even better at fooling them by escaping and, in his case, using a false name.[6] When I got home that night and told Alonso and Julia what had happened, they agreed that the owners were just trying to get my money.[7]

Yet, a number of things make it clear that Salasacas take San Gonzalo's witchcraft very seriously, their skepticism notwithstanding. Above all, most Salasacas still say they believe that San Gonzalo can and does kill people, and some do pay these extremely high prices to have names removed from and entered in the book. For example, when one of the San Gonzalo owners was caught by the police in 1996, she reported that she generally charged from $100 to $150 to have a name removed from the book. The fact that anyone pays that much money—about four to six months' wages—shows that at least some Salasacas deeply believe in San Gonzalo's powers.[8] Even those who saw my experience with San Gonzalo as an exploitative fraud still believed in this witchcraft at another level. Concerned that I had given the owners my real name, Alonoso and Julia said I should have offered a pseudonym, as Jorge did, so that my name wouldn't appear in the book; and they were relieved when I pointed out that my first name is not the same in English as the Spanish translation in my candle and San Gonzalo's book. Yet my story never caused Alonso and Julia to retreat from their beliefs in San Gonzalo; in fact, in the midst of all these discussions, Julia told me another detailed story about someone close to her getting killed by San Gonzalo. She told me this story by way of contrast with my own experience, as well as in contrast with her own prior skepticism. Many Salasacas had similar stories about having discounted San Gonzalo's powers, and later coming to believe in him after a significant personal experience (for example, sudden misfortune, illness, or recovery) reversed their opinions. Even my more skeptical friends without such personal experiences never referred to San Gonzalo as a "stick saint" (caspi santo), the insulting term reserved for saints without any special powers, the ones only made of wood, not real flesh (aicha).

There is no contradiction between such skepticism and faith in San Gonzalo's powers. As shown in classic studies of witchcraft and scientific paradigms (Evans-Pritchard 1976 [1937]; Kuhn 1971 [1962]), most cognitive systems regularly overlook or explain away anomalies in their midst.[9] The first time we get misdiagnosed by a doctor, we don't throw up our arms and exclaim, "I knew it; I knew this whole bio-medical tradition was just a big hoax!" We're more likely to continue believing in the medical system as a whole while blaming the individual doctor as an exceptional case (and then getting revenge through a malpractice suit that makes San Gonzalo's witchcraft look like a nickel-and-dime operation). At a certain point the exceptions, anomalies, and contradictions become overwhelmingly embarrassing to any system, throwing it into question and forcing a search for alternative paradigms. But that crisis point has not been reached in Salasaca. Most Salasacas recognize the potential for abuse by individual practitioners, yet they retain belief in San Gonzalo's powers.

I would characterize Salasacas, then, as having a healthy skepticism toward San Gonzalo's witchcraft, while still taking it quite seriously. I would characterize myself, on the other hand, as the victim of an unhealthy degree of North American skepticism. Unable to get over the feeling that I was set up, I never returned to have my name removed from San Gonzalo's books. I've sometimes wondered, though, whether I did the right thing, especially after one hard-headed, senior anthropologist told me she would have paid the fee, having repeatedly witnessed the devastating effects of witchcraft.

COMMENTARY ON CONFLICT

Contrary to common European/North American assumptions, Salasaca beliefs in San Gonzalo are *not* the product of illiteracy or unfamiliarity with the way "writing really works." Quite the opposite, these beliefs persist precisely because the Salasacas do understand the way writing works: they understand that documentation is intimately connected with power, and their magical beliefs capitalize on that connection, adopting writing for witchcraft purposes. In this sense, the skeptical suggestion that San Gonzalo is an exploitative scam is a central aspect of these beliefs: writing is not just associated with power, but with exploitative power.

This point has to be stressed, since there is a widespread assumption that beliefs in the type of magical literacy analyzed in this book will disappear once literacy rates rise. After I describe San Gonzalo, sometimes the first question people ask me is whether the Salasacas are literate, the premise being (and often explicitly stated) that their magical beliefs will disappear once they grasp writing's "real" (that is, practical) nature. This same premise is found in academic studies, from ethnohistorical accounts of ostensible indigenous amazement at alphabetic literacy due to its novelty to discussions of European reverence for runes.[10] Michael Harbsmeier describes this evolutionary premise as follows: "In other words, it is not writing itself, but its absence, and the fact that it is 'new,' that its use perhaps is still restricted to a few, and that it is not fully understood and developed, that [many assume] explains its ubiquitous superstitious and magical quality" (Harbsmeier 1988:257).

The Salasaca case, however, frustrates this expectation. Even by the 1970s, more than half of Salasacas had acquired basic literacy skills (Instituto Nacional de Estadística y Censos:1985:45), and those percentages continued to climb rapidly through the 1990s—yet beliefs in San Gonzalo's powers remained intact. Even the remaining Salasacas without technical literacy skills were far from ignorant of the way writing works. Like the customers who employ professional scribes in other parts of Latin America (Kalman 1999), these people know a great deal about documentation, even if they can't produce it themselves. Salasacas have been exposed to church and state documentation for nearly five centuries, and they know all too well about its effects, which they have had to study carefully in order to survive. If these witchcraft beliefs were only caused by unfamiliarity with literacy, they would have disappeared long ago. Yet they haven't. These beliefs endure because the conditions of inequality and the connections between archival writing and bureaucratic power that gave rise to them persist.

In the next chapter, I will pinpoint the precise types of documentation that have inspired San Gonzalo, surveying the historical record from the colonial era to the present and narrowing down the types of documentation that are the models for San Gonzalo. For now, it's enough to say that San Gonzalo imitates and comments on the power of church and state documentation, that is, the surveillance systems used by the Catholic Church and Ecuadorian government to identify and control people. The most important types of documentation in this regard are baptism books and Civil Registry documents, such as birth and marriage certificates; other sources include tax records and land titles. The critical power of such documents is to control whether someone exists, as an individual and a social category (a citizen, a Catholic, and so on). If you aren't registered in the state's archives, for example, you simply don't exist, from the state's perspective (Cohn 1990; Corrigan and Sayer 1985; Scott 1988).

But what commentary on such records, and church and state power in general, does San Gonzalo provide? On one level, the commentary is a highly negative one. San Gonzalo is literally killing people, having allied himself with the devil, the source of evil itself. The San Gonzalo owners, like other witches, are singled out for severe punishment in the next life. Having imbibed the Catholic Church's teachings for centuries, Salasacas say that punishments in the next life are meted out in proportion to sin, one of the worst of which is being a witch. People with the average amount of sin merely pass through large frying pans in the underworld when they die, but the witch owners will suffer there for an unbearably long time, if not forever. As one Salasaca woman said, "They have these huge frying pans in the other world, with flames, and everyone is burning, burning. That's where the witch owners will go. They'll just be burning there and they won't be able to get out."[11] Since the models for San Gonzalo are church and state archives, these witchcraft beliefs offer a strong critique of government and religious power, like other "everyday, symbolic resistance" (Scott 1985, 1990) that offers critical views of structures of power.

My interpretation is particularly indebted to Michael Taussig's well-known study, *The Devil and Commodity Fetishism in South America* (1980), which uncovers Colombian and Bolivian critiques of capitalism articulated through fetishistic beliefs, such as devil pacts, money baptism, and mining deities. Following the trail blazed by Taussig, I am also examining indigenous, fetishistic beliefs about domination, while extending the focus on economics to relations with the church and state in Quichua-speaking Ecuador.[12]

The effect of such resistance is hard to measure, since it is notoriously difficult to directly link resistance beliefs to more overt, public acts of disobedience. The Salasacas have never ransacked government tax offices or burned down the church's archives and attributed their actions to San Gonzalo's witchcraft. Nonetheless, San Gonzalo provides a concrete, galling example of church and state abuse, and in doing so, promotes Salasaca consciousness of their disadvantaged position in Ecuadorian society. If saints are often seen as a refuge and last hope, a saint who kills is a slap in the face, a potent indigenous commentary on hypocritical abuse of power. For this reason, "it is impossible to separate veiled symbolic resistance to the ideas of domination from the practical struggles to thwart or mitigate exploitation. Resistance, like domination, fights a war on two fronts" (Scott 1990:188).

Rather than a war against whites per se, San Gonzalo's critique is about ethnicity only insofar as it overlaps with power differences. This is why poor white farmers from the surrounding countryside also believe in San Gonzalo, not just the Salasacas. San Gonzalo beliefs criticize powerful, bureaucratic writing, first and foremost; whites are implicated in this critique only to the extent that they control this type of writing.

But San Gonzalo beliefs do not simply resist outside power. Previous resistance studies have often ridden roughshod over subtle contradictions and ambiguities, too eagerly romanticizing resistance and downplaying internal divisions.[13] It is important, then, to be careful before concluding that San Gonzalo represents a straightforward condemnation of church and state power. Looked at from another perspective, you could even say San Gonzalo does good works. San Gonzalo saves people; he allows victims to get cured when their names are removed from his book. San Gonzalo is not just a witch, but a witch with a saint's background, a witch who can be reasoned with. From the perspective of the victim who has been cured by having his name removed from the books, San Gonzalo is a savior. The San Gonzalo owner even tried to position herself in a helper role, treating Jorge and me amiably and acting concerned that we get ourselves cured. On the other hand, the way the owner later chased us away also suggests this interpretation should not be pushed too far. San Gonzalo's healing only occurs in the negative sense of canceling out his own lethal attacks; he is distinctly unlike other Catholic saints who increase fertility or bring good luck, and his prices are exorbitant.

It gets more complicated when we recall that San Gonzalo acts under the command of individual Salasacas. San Gonzalo is only a hired killer: the initiators of the violence are the Salasacas who first bring the names of their enemies to the owners. Indeed, Salasacas are very clear that people who initiate witchcraft are committing a terrible sin and will be punished for it in the next life, burning in large frying pans and suffering tortures longer than someone with the average amount of sin. The blame has to be shared, albeit not equally with the witch owners, who are more actively and regularly involved in killing people.

Salasacas have tried numerous times to put an end to San Gonzalo's witchcraft, indicating their discontent not just with bureaucratic power but with their own witchcraft practices as well. These attempts to eliminate San Gonzalo reveal a double critique, directed both externally at church and state power and internally at intra-community divisions. A good example is the burning of San Gonzalo in 1992, which occurred after a Salasaca woman protested the large fee being charged for the removal of her name from San Gonzalo's book. Despite the woman's protests, the owner would not lower the price, so the Salasaca woman complained openly at a Salasaca community meeting. With the usual silence about witchcraft broken, others joined in with a chorus of angry resentment. Eventually a group of community leaders tried to negotiate a compromise with the saint owners, but the owners still refused to lower the price or turn over the books, so sometime later an angry group of Salasacas returned to destroy San Gonzalo. The crowd forced its way into the house and removed the San Gonzalo statue, books, and victims' personal belongings. The Ambato police, who had arrived by this point, would not allow these items to be taken back to Salasaca, so they were temporarily stored in the Ambato hospital. About four days later, hundreds of Salasacas and others came to the hospital to witness the public destruction of San Gonzalo and his implements. One leader stood on a balcony, displaying some of the books and personal articles that were found, and, as the crowd cheered, all of these materials were thrown on the ground, doused with gasoline, and burned. The San Gonzalo statue, however, would not burn, supposedly because of its special powers, so it was brought back to the central plaza in Salasaca, where it was chopped with axes into small pieces and then burned.

While impressive, the Salasaca victory over San Gonzalo in 1992 was only temporary. San Gonzalo obviously later regenerated himself: after all, I visited him in 1997 with Jorge, and he was doing fine. In fact, I also visited a resurrected San Gonzalo in 1994, only two years after his burning in the plaza. At that time, I simply went to the main church in the city and began talking with an old woman selling candles near the church steps. After gathering that I wanted to see the "little San Gonzalo," the woman called over a young boy, who told me to start walking down the block by myself, so that we wouldn't be seen leaving the church together. The boy caught up with me at the next block, then guided me to a small house about three blocks behind the church. In a bare outer room, I talked with a woman sitting behind a desk like a secretary, and when I asked whether San Gonzalo had been burned earlier, she acknowledged the incident, but said the statue was put back together with the pieces that were left in the plaza, so now he was fine.[14] San Gonzalo was not dead, after all. In fact, San Gonzalo was killed again in 1996, when two women were arrested and imprisoned for running the operation, yet just a year later my friend Jorge and I found San Gonzalo alive and well.[15] Salasacas acknowledged in 1997 that they heard the witch-saint was back in town, that unfortunately he was not killed for good in 1992, and that he will probably continue to regenerate himself in the future. Judging by San Gonzalo's many resurrections, this seems like a reliable prediction. As far back as anyone can remember, San Gonzalo has always had a history of narrowly escaping angry mobs, only to resurrect himself again shortly afterwards.[16]

This cycle of deaths and resurrections reveals a highly complex—conflictive, ambivalent, intense, and ongoing—relationship between the Salasacas and San Gonzalo. On the one hand, individuals continue visiting San Gonzalo, causing the witch-saint to regenerate. As everyone knows, if there weren't such a demand for San Gonzalo, his business would have died out by now. San Gonzalo therefore highlights internal social divisions and discontent with witchcraft, as in other societies (Brown 1988:117; Brown 1991:400–401).

Though internally divided, the Salasacas are also fierce in their opposition to outsiders when faced with a common enemy—in this case, the white San Gonzalo owners, who exploit with high prices and archival records. This opposition dovetails with other Salasaca public acts of disobedience during this period, such as the patrols organized to resist thefts by nearby whites (see previous chapter). At an even more explicitly political level, the Salasacas participated actively in the national indigenous uprising of 1990, described by a seasoned anthropologist, present at the time, as follows:

> On Sunday, June 3 [1990], Ecuador experienced the first nationwide indigenous uprising in its history. The uprising itself began about 3:00 A.M. in Salasaca (just east of Ambato) and had spread throughout the Sierra by late Sunday night. By Monday morning Riobamba and Latacunga were "occupied" by indigenous people. Ambato was sealed off, and there was no access by major or minor roads between Coast, Sierra, and Upper Amazonia. [Whitten 1996:196–197; see also Dash (ed.) (1997)]

As this quotation indicates, this uprising was unprecedented in Ecuadorian history, and though national in scope, the Salasacas played a crucial role in its inception. By the end of the day, the president of Ecuador agreed to meet with leaders of a national indigenous organization (CONAIE) to discuss their demands, which included return of lands, an end to property taxes, cancellation of all debts, a constitutional designation of Ecuador as a multi-ethnic state, among other benefits for Ecuador's indigenous peoples. The motivations for this uprising reflect complex, multiple forces, many pulsing throughout Latin America at this time (Fischer and McKenna [eds.] 1996; Hill 1996 [ed.]; Rappaport 1994a), but San Gonzalo's witchcraft is part of this complex puzzle. Marching into Ambato to burn the witch's books and blocking off the Ambato road in support of this uprising, the Salasacas recognized and boldly resisted oppression. While you need not say that one event directly caused the other, they clearly belong to a similar pattern and feed off each other, raising awareness of oppression and focusing resentments on dramatic moments that remind Salasacas of their potential power within Ecuadorian society. It is fair to say, then, that San Gonzalo witchcraft represents both an internal and external critique of power.

Notes

1. This sign was written by Devotee Holguer G. B., a church historian, and the sign was erected on May 6, 1999, before which time no church-sanctioned version of San Gonzalo's history was available to visitors to the Church of the Medalla Milagrosa. As of March 2000, the nuns in the church have given out a free, smaller, photocopied version of this history to those who show special interest in San Gonzalo.

2. Some people told me there are various San Gonzalo owners, and, indeed, more recent newspaper reports (discussed below) have noted the emergence of a copy-cat operation, explicitly based on the sisters' operation described here. Still, given the sisters' more long-standing, widespread reputation and my specific experience with them, I focus on them here and the situation in the 1990s.

3. In fact, that's what happened during my earlier visit to San Gonzalo, described further below.

4. No name seemed to be repeated, and I couldn't discern any pattern in the types of people listed (i.e., how sick they were, the type of sickness, etc.).

5. The importance of envy and interpersonal conflict is typical for other forms of witchcraft. For a classic account of witchcraft, see Evans-Pritchard (1976) [1937]; for an excellent, recent study of Andean witchcraft, see Joralemon and Sharon (1993). Like Joralemon and Sharon, I would not automatically assume that witchcraft has positive functions (leveling wealth differences, etc.), since it can exacerbate social tensions as well.

6. On "dissembling behavior" in the face of power among the Coaiquer in Ecuador, see Ehrenreich (1985); for examples from various parts of the world, see Scott (1990).

7. The Salasacas' views seem to overlap with those of upper-class Ecuadorian whites, who, if they had heard of San Gonzalo's witchcraft (many had not), said it was just an exploitative scam (estafa, engaño), a way to make money off the ignorance of the indigenous. The church even posted a sign next to the statue that explicitly expressed this view:

> Respected devotee of San Gonzalo, please do not allow yourself to be fooled by the exploiters who want to create surprises. God is the only one who cures and saves. God is the only giver of all good things. Devotion to San Gonzalo is for good and not for evil. Do not let them fool you if they say that your name is written somewhere else.

8. This was reported in the Ambato daily newspaper (El Heraldo, July 18, 1996:1).

9. See Taussig (1998) for a recent discussion of the inherent relationship between skepticism and magic.

10. The assumption that literacy is perceived in early-contact situations as magical because of its novelty and unfamiliarity is found in numerous accounts (e.g., Axtell 1988; Gelb 1963 [1952]; Olson 1994:28–33; Todorov 1984); see other examples and critical evaluation of them in Harbsmeier (1988:253–256); Kulick and Stroud

(1990:294); and Wogan (1994). In terms of European attitudes toward magical literacy, Bengt Holbek, for example, sees the use of
runes as a transitional stage in the move away from magical beliefs:
"This seems to reflect a transitional attitude towards writing: on the
one hand, the belief of the illiterate in the power of the written word
is retained; on the other, profane writing is well known—the belief
therefore has to be associated with a *special* sort of writing"
(1989:184). Gelb (1963 [1952]:232–235) reveals similar evolutionary
assumptions when he refers to a 1910 English consecration of
Westminster Abbey with special papers as a Tylorian cultural survival,
or, in his own words, as a "curious left-over of the belief in the sacred
character of writing."

11. In a later chapter I provide a detailed description of Salasaca conceptions of the other world, including frying pans and punishments. See
also Lyons (1999:38) for an Ecuadorian highland story about an hacienda owner who gets burned up in the other world as punishment
for his actions on earth.

12. Taussig touches on literacy symbolism in a later work (1987:259–273),
where he again focuses on market relations.

13. Critiques of Taussig (1980) include Gross (1983); McEachern and
Mayer (1986); Platt (1978); Roseberry (1989); Trouillot (1986); and
Turner (1986). For critiques of resistance studies in general, see Abu-
Lughod (1990); Brown (1991, 1996); Fox and Starn (eds.) (1997);
Kaplan and Kelly (1994); and Ortner (1995).

14. The woman indicated that San Gonzalo was in the next room, but,
because I couldn't pay the high fee required, I never got to see the
books or the statue that day.

15. In an article that appeared in the local newspaper (*El Heraldo,* July 18,
1996:1), one of the women described a San Gonzalo operation very
much like the one reported to me by Salasacas: "When the victim had
just barely arrived, they asked his name, and wrote it down in a black
book without the patient realizing it; in this way, later they could say
that, in fact, his name was in the book all along. . . . In the book of
black masses appear the names of the victims and the amount that
they have to pay to save themselves from the witchcraft." According to
the article, this business was recently started by a woman who was

copying the original owners, i.e., the ones I visited in 1997. It's clear that the recent owners have been women, consistent with gender patterns and writing: many secretaries, notary publics, clergy (i.e., the nuns), and virtually all the pre-university teachers whom the Salasacas encounter are female.

16. People say that in the 1940s San Gonzalo was kept in a house on the outskirts of the city, where the soccer stadium now stands, but he later had to escape with his owners just before an angry mob could burn him. He was then resettled next to the marketplace, on the other side of the city, but, once again, sometime in the 1980s, he was forced to escape, this time to a marketplace near the river, not too far from the center of town. The San Gonzalo house I found in 1994 was in a separate location, closer to the town center, so obviously the witch-saint had moved again—and these were just the moves that I was told about or personally witnessed.

3

Sources of Magical Beliefs

So what are the precise sources of beliefs in San Gonzalo, and, for that matter, the other forms of magical literacy found in Salasaca? That is, what are the actual experiences that these beliefs both imitate and comment on? This chapter pinpoints these experiences through a review of the documentation that Salasacas have had most contact with, from the colonial period to the present. This review picks up where the "Introduction" left off by fleshing out the nature of the Salasacas' interethnic relationships, since writing has been at the nexus of so many of the Salasacas' interactions with outsiders, as in other Andean societies (Rappaport 1994a–c, 1998[1990]). It will become clear, for example, that these relationships are as much about power as ethnicity, and that, like other Latin American groups, the Salasacas have not lived an isolated village existence but have been in regular contact with outside authorities.[1]

SOURCES FOR
BELIEFS IN MAGICAL WRITING

At first glance, the most likely models for San Gonzalo are tax records and land titles. Like San Gonzalo's books, these records inspire terrible fear: the former threaten loss of life; the latter threaten loss of land and other resources, the material bases on which the Salasacas sustain themselves. San Gonzalo therefore fits the pattern described by José Sánchez Parga: "Since indigenous farmers have associated writing with power, with forms of domination and exploitation, there appears this fear of the written word, to which is always attributed a hidden threat and a certain fetishism: the fear of taxes, the fear even today of censuses, this rejection most recently of written questionnaires and being investigated" (1983:60). Such fears are paramount for subsistence farmers; hence, Latin American indigenous groups have consistently employed writing to defend their lands.[2] Archival literacy in all three cases—San Gonzalo witchcraft, taxes, and land titles—contains tremendous power, even the power of life and death.

Nonetheless, the importance of titles and taxes per se should not be overemphasized. As we will see further below, the Salasacas have not retained communal land titles, nor have they used titles for individual land possession until recently, if at all. And taxes have not been paid throughout most of the twentieth century. Nor has the census had a major impact: according to most Salasacas, the first time they actually permitted a census was in 2001. Thus, additional factors must be considered to account for contemporary beliefs in San Gonzalo.[3]

An important place to start with is the Civil Registry, a state bureaucracy with which the Salasacas have had extensive contact since its inception in 1901. Throughout the twentieth and into the twenty-first centuries, the Salasacas have been officially required to visit the Civil Registry to acquire certificates of birth, marriage, death, and, more recently, personal identification cards (Flores Freire 1987:8–9). Enforcement of these rules was previously lax, but, at least within the past several decades, most Salasacas have consistently acquired these documents.[4] This change is due not only to tighter enforcement following the Civil Registry Reform Law of 1966, but also the Salasacas' increasing involvement with education and the market economy, which force them into a tight system of interlocking authorization requirements. For example, a Civil Registry birth certificate is needed for a child's baptism, communion, school enrollment, and an identification card. Clients who need updated copies of their certificates come to the Civil Registry office and have the form searched for under the appropriate year and name. For an even longer period, the Catholic

Church has also kept records for baptisms, weddings, and funerals, as well as, more recently, confirmations. Whenever people need a copy of their certificate, most commonly a baptism record for confirmation or marriage, they visit the local church and have that certificate searched for according to the date of the ceremony and the names of the participants.

Thus, San Gonzalo, the church, and the state all maintain archives that facilitate retrieval of information by names and dates.[5] While Salasacas are aware that papers are used to record taxes, by contrast, they have never had regular access to those records. Notarial archives are consulted, but only rarely, in the cases where land sales were previously made outside of the family and the documentation has been lost. So while taxes and titles undoubtedly inspire fear, the more insistent, commonplace reminders of church and state power are these other documents.

The church and state documents also resemble San Gonzalo's books stylistically: all three archives are created with black ink on white, lined paper. The writing particularly resembles "numbered paper" (*papel numerado*, Sp.; *hila rurashca papil*, Q.), a special type of white paper—with consecutive numbers for each line running down the page—that was used throughout the twentieth century for Civil Registry certificates and church documents (see Figure 3.1).[6] Until recently, any client who wanted a certificate from the Civil Registry first had to buy a sheet of numbered paper in a bookstore and bring it back to the Civil Registry, where an official used it to type up the certificate, which the Salasaca client then had to carry to a church or school official. Throughout the twentieth century the Salasacas have therefore had extended, even tactile contact with a type of white, lined paper that closely resembles San Gonzalo's books. The church does not use "numbered paper," nor does it usually give clients any papers to take home, but the church books for retrieving records consist of white, lined paper with black ink, and, before 1955, the church used lined paper instead of standardized forms.

All of these records are bureaucratic, archival documents used to monitor and control the Salasacas—and ultimately *to define personal existence*. Recall or imagine the feeling of going to a state bureaucracy and being told your name is not in the records: it is as if you're being told you don't exist. From the state's perspective, you don't: if you're not in the books, you're outside the system, floating in space. As other research

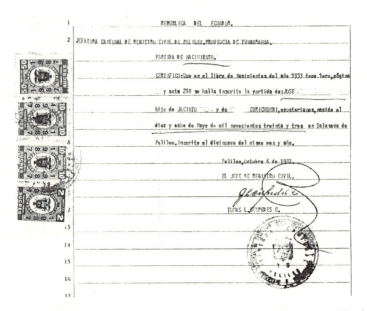

Figure 3.1   A birth certificate on "Numbered Paper," the paper used by the Civil Registry and Catholic church until recently.

shows (see below), the state only recognizes people insofar as they exist in its archives. This may sound like a harsh perspective, and it is, as anyone who has fought to get back into state-defined existence—after being told his or her name does not appear in the election rolls or Motor Vehicles database, for example—can testify. The Ecuadorian state explicitly voiced this perspective in 1995, when it encouraged any Ecuadorians who had not yet registered with the Civil Registry to do so immediately. Toward this end, the government ran a regular series of television commercials explaining that the Registry was temporarily waiving the usual, hefty penalties for not registering. To make the message particularly appealing to young children, the commercial's main character was an animated toucan named "The Best" *(Máximo).* For all his apparent harmlessness, the toucan pithily captured the state's perspective when he flatly told viewers that "If a child is not registered, it's as if he doesn't exist" *(Si el niño no está inscrito, es como si no existiera).*

At first I was surprised to see the state's perspective expressed so candidly, perhaps because I am from a society in which struggles between the state and its citizenry have mostly faded into the background or taken other forms. Most people in the U.S. cannot hope to stay completely outside the state's written surveillance, so they either manipulate state writing for their own purposes (for example, seeking tax loopholes or fake documents), or comply and more or less forget about state documentation. The Salasacas, on the other hand, have developed an acute awareness of the state's perspective, an awareness that crystallizes in a witch-saint that kills you if your name appears in his books. Of course, these views are technically opposites: for the state, death results if you do not appear in the books, whereas, for believers in San Gonzalo, death results if you do appear in the books. But these are just flip sides of the same coin: in both cases, the written, archived name defines existence. From the Salasacas' perspective, once the state is aware of your existence, it may call upon you for the rest of your life to meet its onerous requirements, such as paying taxes or serving in the military. It is much safer to stay off the state's radar screen, which is precisely what the Salasacas have tried to do for as long as possible. The Salasacas are similar to illegal immigrants and unlike citizens who worry when told they do *not* appear in important state records. Either way, the state defines personal existence through its written records.[7] While the Salasacas' awareness of this situation is partly based on their fear of tax records, it is also reinforced by contact with the Civil Registry, contact that has intensified in the second half of the twentieth century. Moreover, their awareness, astutely represented through San Gonzalo, is of an existential nature, not simply a fear of taxes. If taxes are the muscle of the state, Civil Registry documents are its eyes or prison viewing tower (Foucault 1977).

The Civil Registry's power to define acceptable, legal names is particularly important to the Salasacas because of their equation between personal names and individual essence. In healing practices, for example, curers call out surrounding mountains' names to invoke their powers, and patients' names are called to make their souls return to their bodies. Also, a child with the same name as his or her parents or grandparents is referred to as "Old Man" (*Rucu*) or "Old Woman" (*Vija*), reflecting the belief that having the same name creates a special bond between the child and his or her namesake. Salasacas say that an "Old Man" will share the heart and outlook of his father (*Libre shunguda apan, paibug yuyida charinga*), increasing the father and son's chances for harmonious relations. These

"Old" names are common, given endogamous marriage patterns and stress on honoring elder relatives by keeping their memories and first names alive across the generations. The result is a predominance of a limited number of last and first names. Civil Registry documents for 1900–1920 showed that 48.5 percent of male first names consisted of the same four names (Juan, José, Pedro, Manuel), and three names (Rosa, Juana, María) corresponded to 46 percent of the female names.

Partly to prevent the confusion that could result from this degree of identicalness in names and partly for comic effect, most males are known by colorful nicknames like "Guinea Pig Face" *(Cuy Cara)*, "Bishop" *(Obispo)*, and "Rabbit" *(Conejo)*, highlighting some identifiable characteristic or weakness in a person.[8] Nicknames are predominantly assigned to Salasaca males, usually by someone in a group of close male friends in the habit of teasing each other. For example, one male was nicknamed "Baby Bread" *(Hua Hua Tanda)* when he was in his twenties working in a small, three-person (male) "bakery" in Salasaca. Although he received this name because of an ostensibly positive quality rather than a weakness—he was good at making this baby-shaped bread (for a description of which, see Chapter 5)—the joke lies in the incongruity between the images of a full-grown male (now in his thirties) and a small piece of bread named and shaped like a baby. The greater predominance of male nicknames is a result not only of slightly more aggressive male joking patterns, but also gender differences in work habits: men work day in and day out together (usually weaving tapestries in the same house, sometimes with friends) more often than women, who more commonly work in the house with one or two other family members. Nonetheless, women as well as men are familiar with these nicknames. By reinforcing the equation between one's name and personality, these naming practices predispose the Salasacas to accept the state's premise that "If children are not registered, it's as if they don't exist."

Following recent research (see below), it is also important to view Civil Registry documentation as a state ritual. A good example is the marriage process that takes place on Saturday nights at the Civil Registry in Salasaca. Those who plan to get married show up with a small group, including two witnesses (who cannot be immediate family members), and (usually) the parents on both sides, and several other close family members, who will also attend the party that takes place at the husband's house after the legal inscription. But the key ritual moment is the signing of the marriage forms, which, according to the Chief of the Civil Registry, is often recorded with photographs. A Salasaca friend of the groom videotaped a wedding ceremony I attended in 2002, and it was interesting to see that he did not record the preparation of the papers but filmed the moments of signing in their entirety, zooming in so the screen is filled with images of pens, hands, and signatures. When we returned to the house for the party, we were asked, "Did you sign well?" This is a ritual that changes one's social status from single to married, and the ritual centers on the signing of documents.

This Civil Registry's change of social status is especially important because many couples do not get married in the church for one to four years after the Civil Registry ceremony, due to the greater cost of a church celebration (in 2002, approximately $1,000 as opposed to $100 for the Civil Registry). Although the Civil Registry does not completely replace the church, it does take on religious tones. As we left the Civil Registry in 2002, the other witness said to the father of the bride, "Well, now we're godparents" *(compadregunami tucunchi).* And the Civil Registry Chief, like a priest, gave the young couple a sermon on the seriousness of marriage and their obligations.

This chief was a fellow Salasaca, but until this man started running the Civil Registry in Salasaca over eight years ago, many Salasacas experienced gruff, if not insulting, treatment from white Civil Registry bureaucrats in Pelileo. Alonso's wife, Julia, for example, tells of literally being slapped in the face by a white attendant because she was crying during her first marriage (before marrying Alonso). And another Salasaca man, Rumiñahui Masaquiza Masaquiza, describes his frustrated attempts to have his son registered under his own Quichua name as essentially a slap in the face. He writes, "When the functionary had heard my request, he reprimanded me, saying 'What is this bullshit?' I explained that there was a decree to that effect, and he answered me by saying he didn't want to hear anything about that, and that I should leave the office and go talk with the Provincial Director" (Masaquiza Masaquiza 1995:223). But even if the treatment is polite, the Civil Registry always has the power, like the church, to define names, marriages, and other social identities.

Not only is the state like the church, but the reverse is also true: the Catholic church also defines personal existence through archival surveillance and religious rituals and beliefs. Baptism, in particular, defines Christian identity, since you are not a Christian, according to the church, until you have been baptized. Baptism is the first sacrament, the rite of passage that brings you into the Christian community and separates you from the pagans. As Stutzman (1981:82) notes, "Baptism is the basic rite, the sign that the creature has become human by having entered the moral universe organized by the Creator. Unbaptized children, like the most savage of the pagan Amazonian tribes, are *aucas,* which is to say, amoral beings for whom right and wrong have neither meaning nor consequence." Morgan (1998) finds similar beliefs among mestizos in northern Ecuador, as does Smith (2002:174–175) for indigenous Saraguros: "It's common in Saraguro to use the word 'Christian' as a synonym for 'human.' This is why there's a phrase 'edible for Christians,' which implies a contrast with food that is for animals." These descriptions apply equally well to the Salasacas. Having adopted the church's teachings, Salasacas even say among themselves that an unbaptized child is a "pagan" *(auca)* or "child of the devil" *(diablobug mara).*[9] As Alonso noted, his grandparents used to say that during the long-ago days *(Urdimal Tiempo),* if you did not have a baby baptized, he would become a dog, monkey, or some other animal. But what prevents a child from becoming a child of the devil is that his or her name is entered in the church's baptism books; without that written name, the church does not officially recognize that the baptism took place, and the church will not permit the unbaptized to receive other sacraments. The Salasacas are reminded of this every time they go to the church for a later sacrament (confirmation, marriage, funeral) and have the baptismal record searched. Such experiences drive home the power of archival books—books with the power to decide whether you exist as a Christian and whether you are going to heaven or hell—and underpin beliefs in San Gonzalo.

Indeed, the Salasacas themselves confirm that San Gonzalo's book is modeled on the Civil Registry and baptism books. When I asked one woman what type of writing San Gonzalo's book most closely resembles, she said the following:

Well, the Registro Civil has lined paper, too, and it's just all names, one after another. San Gonzalo's house is just like that. And the baptism books are like that, too. And God's book is exactly like that, too. Let's make a comparison. When we're born, we all go to the Civil Registry, all of us; whether we're indigenous or whites *(chologuna gaquish)*, we all have to go there, to that house for the counting of the citizens.[10] We also go there when we get married. So, even if we never went to Ambato, when we go to get the identity card, they look in the computer and see that we're married. Or if you go to the church and tell them your name, they can look for the paper and know when you were born. And San Gonzalo is exactly like the Civil Registry and the baptism books. And God's book, too. Absolutely everything is there, every single name, whether it's a man's or woman's. God will look in that book and see everything, and San Gonzalo's book is the same way.

She highlights, above all, the similarities between the Civil Registry, baptism books, and San Gonzalo's book in terms of their archival function: their recording of names and dates, the image of control presented by their total comprehensiveness ("Absolutely everything is there, every single name, whether it's a man's or woman's"). She also draws a comparison with God's book, which is the topic of the next chapter. Without getting ahead of the story, it's fair to say that the precise similarity between three different magical name lists (San Gonzalo's book, God's book, and the list of souls, the subject of Chapter 5), together with the Salasacas' explicit recognition of these similarities and consistent comparisons with the Civil Registry and baptism books, add to the evidence that the latter are the main sources of beliefs in San Gonzalo.

Other Salasacas also consistently compared San Gonzalo's book with church and Civil Registry books: "It [San Gonzalo's book] must be like a baptism book"; "They say it's like the big books the church has"; "They say they [the owners] have one of those big books, like they have when you go to the Civil Registry. It's like when you go to get your birth certificate and they put your name in the book." Although nobody spontaneously compared San Gonzalo's book with tax records, land titles, or censuses, most were willing to go along with me when I suggested this possibility, sometimes noting that land titles, in particular, also get archived in big books. As one middle-aged man put it, "Yes. The land writing also stays there, archived in a big book" *(Ari. Achpa escrituranaga chibi saquirin, archivashca, shug rucu librobi)*. Ultimately, there is no reason to posit one or two supreme sources for Salasaca beliefs in magical writings. While certain possibilities can be eliminated (for example, newspapers) and the field narrowed down to major influences, there will always be a range of associations with multiple types of literacy. Salasacas presumably point to Civil Registry documents and baptism books most readily because they have had the most consistent, recent contact with them, but other types of writing, such as tax records, land titles, and censuses, can also be encompassed by San Gonzalo's symbolism.[11]

TRIBUTE AND TAXES

From the start of the colonial period in the 1530s to the present, records of tribute and taxes have figured prominently in Salasaca experiences with literacy, as in other Andean societies (Rappaport 1998[1990], 1994c). Tribute to the state was largely exacted through the *encomienda* system during the colonial period. In theory, this system required indigenous people to make annual payments to an individual Spaniard known as an *encomendero,* who in return was expected to provide protection and Christianization. In reality, minimal Christianizing took place for centuries; the protection most needed was from the encomenderos themselves; and the tribute, initially a share of the agricultural yield, was soon exacted in labor on the encomendero's properties. The Salasacas could not have escaped the abuses of one of the nearby Pelileo encomiendas during the first centuries of colonial rule.[12] And they must have had contact with various encomienda papers, including detailed surveys *(visitas)* of demography, residence, governance, and tribute (Guevara-Gil and Salomon 1994).

Although the *encomienda* system was officially abolished in 1718, indigenous people continued paying tribute in various forms through the post-1830, independence period (Moreno Yánez 1983:100–105). Under the *mita,* they were obligated to render labor to the Spanish Crown, sometimes absent from their communities for six months at a time for this purpose. The Pelileo indigenous people, in particular, were sent to work in distant gold mines (Guevara 1945:85). Salasacas also paid the church with the *diezmo,* a tax consisting of 10 percent of agricultural produce, used to support local clergy within the Pelileo "religious center" *(reducción)* established in 1570 (Guevara 1945:84–87).

In reaction to these burdensome taxes, there were many indigenous rebellions (Coba Robalino 1929:205–221), and writing was consistently a central target. In 1898, for example, an angry mob burned all the Píllaro municipal archives in the course of a five-day uprising against new taxes.[13] Based on testimonies from eyewitnesses, José Maria Coba Robalino graphically describes the scene as follows:

> In the central plaza was heard the cry, "Hurrah for the sacking!" And, in effect, the farmers and Indians attacked the stores where they sold alcohol, food, and clothes. Soon the Indians and many farmers became drunk, and, thinking that if the Municipal Decree were burned up the new tax would be eliminated, they started to loot the Municipal Center and all its offices. In the plaza of San Juan they formed a giant bonfire and into it they threw every last paper, old and new, of the Archives of the Municipal Center, of the Political Headquarters, of the Police, Mayor, Courts, etc., as they had attacked the houses of Merizalde and Miranda [two tax collectors]. All of the bundles of legal dossiers and papers were reduced to ashes, destroying precious historic documents, both ancient and modern, including original legal Minutes from 1700 onward. [Coba Robalino 1929:376]

After burning the archives, the crowd then tried to kill the *quillcas*— the scribes and legal experts who acted as intermediaries between indigenous people, whites, courts, and state bureaucracies.[14] Coba Robalino (1929:213) describes other cases where *quillcas* were murdered, and Guevara-Gil and Salomon (1994:23) cite similarly intense conflict over taxation in eighteenth-century, highland Ecuador, describing it as "the most bloodthirsty ethnic warfare Ecuador ever saw." After reading about rebellions such as these, nobody can doubt that writing involved with taxes and legal matters was the object of intense resentment by indigenous, disenfranchised farmers.

Governments in the post-independence period largely continued the colonial period's heavy taxation. Indigenous people still had to pay diezmos as late as 1883, and they contributed their labor to various public works projects and were threatened with military service and sales taxes, which led to additional revolts (Fuentealba M. 1983:56–73; Guerrero 1994).

The Salasacas understandably don't remember the details of this history, but most have a definite sense that whites have been extracting taxes and work from them since the Conquest period, that record keeping has been an integral part of this oppression, and that Salasacas have been constantly fleeing or taking stands against this oppression. The best examples are reports from those who have died and returned to life, who say the first stage of the underworld hell is a large hacienda or workshop, where the dead souls work as punishment and penance for their sin.[15]

LAND TITLES AND CENSUSES

Though Salasacas say their territory used to be more extensive, they have never been incorporated into an hacienda over the years. This has not been achieved, however, by preserving a colonial, communal land title, or at least if such a title ever existed, it was lost over the years, perhaps in the 1797 earthquake or one of the sackings of colonial archives. Would-be invaders have been repelled through intimidation and annual rituals marking off the village borders (Corr 2000:141–145; cf. Rappaport 1994a).

Until recently, individual Salasacas also made minimal use of writing to ensure personal land ownership. The majority of Salasacas told me they never had land titles forty years ago; they said they simply handed on land within the usual inheritance rules, bilaterally and equally among a parent's children, male and female.[16] Salasacas also managed to reject efforts by the Pelileo municipal government to charge land sales taxes. In a 1913 report, for example, the Political Chief of Pelileo complained that he couldn't carry out a land census or charge taxes since the Salasacas refuse to give their names and they "force the officials to take flight by threatening to kill them" (cited in Poeschel-Renz 2001:75–76).

Nonetheless, by the end of the twentieth century, the Salasacas started acquiring land writings at a growing pace, not just to replace writings lost in the 1949 earthquake but in response to more recent pressures. Documentation is required, for example, for lands used as collateral for bank loans. More importantly, the municipal government announced in 1988 that the Salasacas' "land writings" are not legally valid, even if they were written up by notary publics; land ownership, they said, is only ensured through the National Registry of Property (where taxes are also charged). Not surprisingly, the Salasacas are not eager to pay land taxes, especially since they do not receive any particular benefits from the municipality, but recently more and more Salasacas have started to use the Registry, willing to incur taxes for the security afforded.

Land titles are, in short, part of a cat-and-mouse struggle between the Salasacas and the state over taxes. Fear of taxes taints most associations with government documentation, especially censuses that attempt to systematically count people and possessions. Unconfirmed stories circulate of Salasacas physically harming census enumerators; whether true or not, such stories help to perpetuate government officials' fears of Salasacas.[17] Certainly Salasacas resisted the census during the twentieth century. Although a national census has been carried out in Ecuador roughly once every decade since 1950 (Zurita Herrera 1992; Instituto Nacional de Estadística y Censos 1991), most Salasacas say that the first time they ever permitted a census was in 2001. Visible evidence of this census remained in 2002, when I often saw green stickers on doors, stating in capital letters "CENSUS COMPLETED" (see Figure 3.2). Salasacas told me that previously, though, everybody hid from or tried to scare away the census enumerators, for fear they would collect taxes or even take children. This is the way one middle-aged farmer put it:

> My grandparents had said the census is coming, and because of it the whites will fall into some sort of misfortune. And maybe that's the meaning of Tungurahua exploding? [A nearby volcano became active in 2000, and forced the evacuation of a predominantly white town.] My grandparents also said that the census people would take one child from every family. So everyone was afraid of the census, and they sent them running away. But now we're not afraid of the taxes.

The censuses' influence on the Salasacas has been minimized, though, partly because they weren't successfully carried out until 2001, and, unlike

Figure 3.2   Sticker on a house door: "CENSUS COMPLETED."

other cases (cf. Cohn 1990; Kertzer and Arel [eds.] 2002; et al.), they have not introduced particularly novel or controversial social categories. Ethnicity is not even recorded on the census, and most groups are categorized according to age and gender, which are already salient local categories. But if the census does not have the effect on group identity found in previous studies, it is crucial as another example of state attempts to track, monitor, and control Salasacas through archival documents. As Julia said, "they do the census all over Ecuador, everywhere, wherever you're from, because they want to know exactly the right numbers."

CHURCH LITERACY AND EDUCATION

Writing has also been a central aspect of white—European-based, Christian—identity from the Conquest to the present. Christianity is, after all, a religion of the book, distinguished by the Bible's sacred texts and teachings. Thus, colonial Spanish writers justified Pizarro's conquest by saying the Inca Atahualpa rejected Christianity when he threw a Bible on the ground (Abercrombie 1998:164–167; MacCormack 1988; Seed 1991). And just as the Spanish colonialists interpreted lack of Christianity as a mark of "barbarism," they applied the same logic to the absence of alphabetic writing: "The lack of alphabetic writing was one of the most significant trademarks, next to lack of clothing and the eating of human flesh, in the construction of the image of the Amerindians during the sixteenth and early seventeenth centuries" (Mignolo 1992:312; see also Harbsmeier 1985:72; Mignolo 1995:29–67).

Probably no Salasaca is aware of the historical roots of these European-language ideologies, but Salasacas certainly associate the Bible with Christianity and "civilization." They have been Christianized since at least 1570, when Pelileo was established as a religious center. For centuries, visits to the Pelileo church were primarily limited to major sacraments and festivals, but early in the twentieth century, the church in Pelileo started showing an increasingly active interest in the Salasacas.[18] Intense involvement began in 1945, when a group of Colombian Catholic nuns, the Hermanas Lauritas, constructed a church in the center of Salasaca and established a permanent mission there.[19] Although to this day attendance at weekly mass is still minimal outside of major fiesta days, a mark of the church's growing strength is that recently they were able to instate a rule that Salasacas must complete a two-month catechism course before being married. As a result of these various efforts, almost all Salasacas today sincerely identify themselves as Catholics, expressing belief in God, the afterlife, and notions of sin, blending these beliefs, in typical syncretic fashion, with historically indigenous beliefs. Salasacas also believe that non-Christians are "savages" (aucaguna), and they view the Bible as a symbol of Christianity.

In addition, the church has been closely associated with literacy ever since the nuns opened a primary school and adult literacy center in 1947. Before that time, there were no schools in Salasaca itself, apart from a short-lived one started in 1930 by Hilario Chango, who is said to be the first Salasaca to have learned to read and write.[20] Even through the 1950s and 1960s, and despite calls by Hilario Chango and other leaders for local schooling, Salasaca elders objected that schooling would make the kids lazy or turn them into thieves. The Salasacas were well aware of writing's importance as an instrument of power, but not everyone felt compelled to acquire literacy skills individually. Literacy skills were not needed for subsistence farming, and, when particular legal situations arose, they could rely on intermediaries who were familiar with Spanish and legal, literate conventions. Aside from the costs of school supplies and lost farm labor, the nuns' education programs also threatened indigenous culture, with their attempts to eradicate "paganism" and insistence that students have short hair, shoes, and European/North American dress (Poeschel-Renz 2001:115–124). To overcome initial resistance, the nuns had to offer gifts to families, followed by threats of police reprisal for non-attendance. Today, however, such prodding is no longer necessary, because, despite certain misgivings, parents willingly and increasingly send their children to school. The town has eight thriving elementary schools and a bilingual high school.

Changing attitudes toward education have gone hand in hand with changes in economic activities. Over the course of the twentieth century, the Salasacas have moved increasingly toward a blend of subsistence agriculture and commercial work, especially due to population growth, land scarcity, and worsening conditions caused by the earthquake of 1949. The weaving trade has emerged as a major source of supplemental (and, in some cases, primary) income, to such an extent that most homes have a tapestry loom, and male children master weaving skills before they are teenagers. These weavings are sold to tourists passing through Salasaca, international exporters, and to intermediary vendors in Otavalo.[21] Many young males also find work in construction and the tourist trade in the Galápagos Islands or Ambato. With the men absent for long periods, women increasingly control agricultural production, though some also work in nearby cities as housekeepers and cleaners.[22]

But while Salasacas have increasing contact with literacy through education, the major sources for magical beliefs remain the church and state documentation discussed earlier.

THEORETICAL CONTEXT

The San Gonzalo case is particularly interesting, from a theoretical perspective, because it shows that this native group shares recent researchers' views of state documentation. Philip Corrigan and Derek Sayer, for example, advance a view of documentation as a routine by which the state asserts its power in a tangible, material form (Corrigan and Sayer 1985:21), with "the ability to define social identities and categories from the state's perspective" (Corrigan and Sayer 1985:140–141). It is fair to make this point with regard to "the state" in general, for, as James Scott (1988) makes clear, documentation practices are characteristic of all states, modern and colonial, European/ North American and non-European/North American. In practices ranging from cadastral surveys and the standardization of surnames to the registration of land tenure, Scott shows the modern state engaged in a project of "legibility and simplification": that is, the reduction of complex, fluid social realities to simplified categories that can be recorded and monitored. And Scott notes, as Corrigan and Sayer do, that the state does not simply document social reality, but in doing so, creates it as well.

Other studies have shown this process at work with the state census. Bernard Cohn, for example, argues that, by posing questions about caste, population, and other matters, the colonial census in India raised self-consciousness of cultural categories: "the census was one of the situations in which Indians were confronted with the question of who they were and what their social and cultural systems were" (1990:248). Armando Guevara-Gil and Frank Salomon (1994) have also interpreted colonial tours of inspection in Latin America as bureaucratic theater that created "Indians" and other social categories, and other studies in a wide range of contexts have shown similar effects.[23]

Reading all these authors, it is clear that state documentation is a topic of growing interdisciplinary interest—and justifiably so. Yet the virtually exclusive focus on government elites and official discourse in this work leaves room for further investigation. Rarely has the focus been on the perspectives of "ordinary" non-elites, as the authors themselves explicitly acknowledge. Corrigan and Sayer state that "the very focus of our narrative—on that 'political nation', on 'history from above'—constantly risks 'overlooking' exactly those outside and below" (Corrigan and Sayer 1985:12). And Cohn says that the effects of the Indian census were limited to its enumerators: "I don't think that the act of a census enumerator asking a question of a peasant contributed too much to the process [of objectification]. . . . If there was a direct effect of the census on the mass of the Indian population, it was on the enumerators" (1990:248).[24] In light of this imbalance, authors have recently called for more ethnographic investigation of state documentation: "Sorely needed are more ethnographic efforts at examining the workings of state agencies of various kinds—from legislatures to census-takers— in their interactions with each other and with the people under their surveillance" (Kertzer and Arel 2002:6).[25] Accordingly, rather than infer the effects of documentation on non-elites, I have made this the central topic of my investigation. Without such ethnographic investigation, we run the risk of assuming that state documentation has the same controlling, consciousness-raising, legibility effects in every culture—in other words, the risk of technological determinism, in which print technology becomes an autonomous, invariant, universal force in social relations. It may be that cross-cultural similarities are found in perceptions of documentation, but this can't be determined a priori, without empirical investigation. And certainly the nuances of each culture's responses to documentation can't be known without ethnographic research.

Such an approach draws on a well-established tradition of ethnographic research on literacy, often referred to as the "ideological model of literacy" or the "New Literacy Studies." These studies explore the way literacy is shaped by cultural context and power relations, demonstrating that literacy is not a neutral, universal phenomenon.[26] I have been inspired by this perspective, as well as recent emphasis in anthropological linguistics on native conceptions of language or "language ideologies" (Irvine 1992; Parmentier 1993; Silverstein 1979; Woolard and Schiefflin 1994). Another major influence has been researchers of Latin American literacy, notably Joanne Rappaport, Serge Gruzinksi, Walter Mignolo, and Thomas Abercrombie,[27] who have demonstrated beyond a doubt the centrality of the written word in indigenous cultures, particularly the importance of legal documentation in struggles with the state over territorial rights. As Rappaport puts it, "It is more properly within the legal document . . . that the impact of literacy among Andean native peoples is most clearly evident, for it is with this type of writing that aboriginal communities came most frequently into contact. In other words, from the colonial period to the present, the legal document has constituted the major genre of written expression and of communication across the two cultures" (1994c:272).

Twenty years ago, in the absence of such research, a study like mine would not have been conceived. The difference, however, is that I focus on the relationship between identity categories and state and church documentation, whereas these Latin American works concentrate more on historical consciousness and oral-literate influences. And while these studies greatly improve upon research on state documentation that hovers at the level of official discourse, they still do not fully explore the perspectives of ordinary, non-elite groups: instead, they focus on a small group of indigenous, literate specialists who act as intermediaries with church and state bureaucracies.[28] This study, by contrast, concerns the full community.

The upshot is an intimate sense of Salasaca perspectives. Like the native Andean understanding of Marxist theory analyzed by Michael Taussig (1980), the San Gonzalo beliefs reveal how much one indigenous group has understood and taken to heart documentation's power, particularly its capacity to define identity.

Notes

1. For related accounts of other Latin American societies, see Abercrombie (1998); Rappaport (1994a–c, 1998[1990]); Urban and Sherzer (eds.) (1991). When describing recent Salasaca history, I rely on Salasaca recollections, augmented with dates and other details from written reports that supply a sense of magnitude and chronology. I don't dwell on pre–twentieth-century events beyond the reach of living Salasaca memories, yet I consider such background if it shapes Salasacas' current literacy associations. Since archival sources don't usually mention Salasaca by name, this history is largely based on histories of towns like Pelileo, the town Salasaca has been historically attached to through state and church relations.

2. See Condori Chura and Ticona Alejo (1992); Gruzinski (1993[1988]); and Rappaport (1990[1998]), (1994a).

3. I am focusing on San Gonzalo beliefs in the second half of the twentieth century, especially the 1990s, the time during which most of my fieldwork was carried out. Elders told me that San Gonzalo has always existed, that even their grandparents talked about him, so he has clearly been around

since at least the turn of the century. Certainly during earlier periods other forms of writing may have been more important than those discussed below, and San Gonzalo beliefs may have accordingly taken a different form. San Gonzalo is said by the nuns to have been the patron saint of this church since the colonial period (though the current church structure was only built in 1902). It's possible that beliefs in San Gonzalo's witchcraft stretch back to the colonial period, but for obvious reasons this sort of information does not appear in the church archives or histories.

4. For example, there was a sign in July 2002 on the door of the Civil Registry in Salasaca stating that you have to get your child baptized within thirty days or you'll have to pay a fine of $30. Thus, the 1995 campaign to make sure all children get registered (referred to below) has continued, with increasing success. Whereas some people told me that thirty years ago they wouldn't get their children registered until they were four to seven years old, the current (2002) Chief of the Civil Registry in Salasaca told me that most Salasacas now know about the potential fines and therefore have their children registered within a month of birth. See also Belote Smith (2002:166) on late inscriptions in Saraguro in the 1970s.

5. Not all of the San Gonzalo books that I examined contained dates, and even the ones that did only contained the year (written on the inside cover of the book), not specific dates for individual entries. Significantly, though, most Salasacas believe that the books always contain dates.

6. "Numbered paper" was used for certificates since the Civil Registry's inception in 1901 until 1985, when other types of paper were introduced. From 1985 to 1995, the standard Registro Civil paper was a type of blank, bond paper (*papel bon*, Sp. and Q.), and in 1996 the Civil Registry started using special, standardized forms. The Civil Registry books for certificates contain forms, but not numbered paper. These forms, which also follow a linear format, with dotted lines where the information is to be entered, have not changed much since 1901, except that in 1966 the birth certificate forms added a section for the child's fingerprint.

7. Constance Sutton (personal communication, August 1, 2002) notes that, similarly, the Yoruba of Nigeria refused until recently to allow census officials to enumerate the names and birth dates of individuals in a compound, a refusal based on a pre-colonial separation between the rights of (city-)states and local lineages.

8. Because the equation between names and personality is very common, if not universal, in other parts of the world, (e.g., Sutton 1998:173–201), I don't belabor this point.

9. Another name for an unbaptized child is *na rij cachij carishca mara,* literally, "a kid who has not yet been fed some salty food"; in other words, there has not yet been the post-baptism party in which the parents of the child give (salty) food to the godparents and other guests. An unbaptized child is also commonly called "not-yet-named child" *(mana shutichishca mara).* As Belote Smith (2002:175) notes, Amazon tribes like the Shuar can be seen as baptized and Catholic, but not fully civilized or Christian.

10. In this case, the woman refers to the Civil Registry as "that house for the counting of citizens" *(chi ciudadano cuentarina huasi),* which is an interesting phrase, given its focus on both counting and the nation.

11. Given the pervasiveness of both church and state documentation and name-soul equations, it's not surprising to find similar notions of writing sorcery in other times and places (see Skar 1994:273; Wogan 1994:408–411). By contrast, see Rappaport's discussion of Mayan love letters, used not for sorcery but to "wrest power from dominant groups" (1992:124).

12. As Christiana Borchart de Moreno (1983:149) notes, "we still don't have studies detailed enough to allow the pinpointing of the *encomiendas* and rural properties," largely because the encomienda concessions make imprecise references to borders and locations. In addition, these concessions do not always name the relevant indigenous groups. Darío Guevara (Guevara 1945:83–84) refers to Pelileo encomiendas from the late sixteenth century, but doesn't mention the Salasacas. My own inspection of the Quito Libros de Cabildo also failed to turn up any such references. Other investigators (Choque Quispe 1992:102; Corr 2000:15; Costales 1959:18) have similarly noted a dearth of references to Salasacas in the archival record.

13. See Stark (1985b) for an analysis of women's prominent roles in such rebellions. Though Coba Robalino's descriptions apply to Píllaro, an area near Salasaca, I rely on them here, since they are more detailed than those of Guevara (1945:107–111), who does, however, note that the same rebellions occurred in Pelileo.

14. In the past, the term *quillca* meant alphabetic writing, painting, and the scribes who mastered (legal) literacy. The term *quillca* is still used in some parts of the Andes today (see Condori Chura and Ticona Alejo 1992;

Stark and Muysken 1977:53), but Salasacas now commonly use Quichuaized versions of Spanish terms for writing: namely, *escribina* or *iscribina* (Q.), taken from *escribir* (Sp.); or *apuntana* (Q.), from "to note" *(apuntar).* Similar terms are used in Quichua dialects spoken throughout highland Ecuador, with *iscribina* being the most prevalent (Stark and Muysken 1977:52). The Salasacas also use *yanaquina* (literally, "to make black") to refer to legal writing. Extended meanings of the word *quillca* reflect colonial language planning in which alphabetic writing and realistic pictorial representation were conflated (Mignolo 1995; Rappaport and Cummins 1994).

15. See also Corr (2000:182–216), Lyons (1998), and the later chapter on God's book.

16. Others, however, reported using "land writings" or "land contracts" *(achpa escriturana, achpa contrato)* in the past because they wanted more security, or because they were buying or selling land outside normal patterns of family inheritance. There were two types of writings. The first was a simple contract written up by a non-official person, usually a poor white literate neighbor or godparent; the contract included essential information, such as names, dates, amounts paid, and the thumbprints of the buyer and seller. The second type was written (or typed) by a notary public *(notario, escribano)* in a nearby city, with two or more pages of formal legal language. Buyers and sellers retained copies of these papers in their homes (usually in chests or in the roof), and the notary publics kept archived copies of their transactions. Most extant writings of both types were lost, however, in the 1949 earthquake that swallowed up Salasaca homes and most of Pelileo, the nearby town where notary titles were archived.

17. A number of other indigenous groups killed enumerators during the Agriculture and Livestock Census of 1962 (Albornoz Peralta 1971:87; Fuentealba M. 1983:66). Casagrande (1977:88) also mentions "legends" that the Salasacas killed a census taker, though I never encountered any Salasacas who would confirm these legends; most simply said the census takers were scared away with threats. Other municipal taxes do not affect the Salasacas, such as the sewer tax (no sewer system exists in Salasaca) and a tax for Pelileo market stalls (Salasacas do not generally use the stalls). Many negotiations undoubtedly have also occurred in the safer arena of non-public "hidden transcripts" (Scott 1990). Lynn Hirschkind

(1995:333–339), for example, describes the ingenious tactics used by Ecuadorian Cañar Indians to evade colonial taxes, including everything from forging baptismal records to the taking of Spanish names (see also Guevara-Gil and Salomon 1994).

18. In 1921 a Mass was given in Salasaca every fifth Sunday, and in 1939 a catechism visit was instated by the Pelileo priest every Thursday. These changes are reported in the archival records of the Catholic church in Pelileo, specifically the "Autos de Visitas Pastorales" for 1921 and 1939. Although these records start in 1885, the first specific mention of Salasaca appears in 1921. I am grateful to Rachel Corr for locating these documents and allowing me to copy them.

19. Although the nuns themselves date their arrival to 1945, a Salasaca Cabildo secretary, who was alive at that time, noted that the nuns arrived in August of 1946 (Poeschel-Renz 2001:122, note 177).

20. Both Carrasco (1982:25–26) and Poeschel-Renz (2001:122) cite reports, from Salasacas and a Pelileo priest, that Hilario Chango was the first Salasaca to read and write. In the 1990s, I also heard such reports. During the colonial period, Salasaca caciques were probably also familiar with testaments (Salomon 1988), court sentences, legislation, and, in the early sixteenth century, possibly education in Spanish literacy (see Adorno [ed.] 1982; Coba Robalino 1929:240; Ramón Valarezo 1991: 354–356; Rappaport 1994c). Others may have also been intermediaries familiar with Spanish and legal, literate conventions. These types of Salasaca literacy were not mentioned in characterizations I heard of Hilario Chango as the first literate Salasaca.

21. For excellent discussions of Otavalo tourist commerce and social relations, see Colloredo-Mansfield (1999) and Meisch (2002).

22. For details about these economic changes, see Carrasco (1982); Choque Quispe (1992); and Poeschel Rees (1985). Even with long absences, Salasacas have not developed an epistolary tradition, preferring to rely on phone calls and personal visits (cf. Besnier 1995; Skar 1994).

23. In a recent edited volume, *Census and Identity* (Kertzer and Arel [eds.] 2002), David Kertzer and other contributors synthesize the work of previous authors, adding rich cross-cultural, historical perspectives on the census. Other major works on the census include Appadurai (1993); Hirschman (1987); and Urla (1993). For reviews of research on state

documentation, see Foster (1991:244–247); Kertzer and Arel (2002); and Mathur (2000). For an interesting anthropological exploration of some of these ideas, see Foster (2002).

24. Cohn is right to point out that these census enumerators were a "highly significant group as they were literate and educated" (Cohn 1990:248), and the eventual politicization of the census (Cohn 1990:250) suggests that its importance was growing. Nonetheless, the fact remains that Cohn focuses on elites, not subaltern groups, as is the case in most such studies. Making a comparison with Cohn, Jacqueline Urla, for example, writes:

> He [Cohn] suggests that it was probably the enumerators, rather than the whole population, who became most directly engaged with this mode of self-knowledge. It would seem reasonable to assume that the statistical objectification of language use in Usurbil [Basque territory] also had its greatest impact on the survey-takers themselves. However, one would need further ethnographic data to determine how both activists and nonactivists interpreted the survey. [Urla 1993:838, note 18]

25. As Kertzer and Arel (2002:36, note 3) point out, Michael Herzfeld (1992) provides an ethnographic study of bureaucracy. His ethnography does not focus, however, on documentation per se, and it is carried out in a Greek cultural context. In an earlier work (1987:39–41), Herzfeld does mention that writing is central to the symbolism of power and identity in modern Greece, so that regardless of actual literacy skills, Greek villagers will refer to the more powerful European community, Greek elites, and foreign ethnographers as "literate," while they call themselves and their Turkish neighbors "illiterate." Guevara-Gil and Salomon also include native reactions to the imperial "visits," especially in their discussion of resistance efforts (1994:23–24).

26. See, for example, Barton and Hamilton (1998); Besnier (1995); Gee (1996 [1990]); Graff (1979); Heath (1983); Messick (1993); Street (1984, 1993); and Wagner (1993); for reviews, see Collins (1995); Gee (1986); and Street (1999). Initially developed as a reaction against the technological determinism of "Great Divide" theories (e.g., Goody 1977; cf. Goody 2000), these studies have shown, for example, that the presumed relation between intelligence and literacy is ideologically tied to middle-class,

Western notions of essay-text literacy (Street 1984, 1999), literacy campaigns are rooted in local cultural contexts and power struggles (Arnove and Graff 1987; Street 1984:Chapters 7–8), and literacy instruction may perpetuate social stratification (Gee 1996; Graff 1979).

27. See Rappaport (1987, 1992, 1994a–c, 1998 [1990]), Gruzinski (1993), Mignolo (1995, 1992); and Abercrombie (1998). In addition to the works on literacy and memory discussed below, see, for example, Adorno (ed.) (1982); Bloch (1993); Boone and Mignolo (eds.) (1994); Guss (1986); Shryock (1997); and Sutton (2001). Of course other anthropological works (e.g., Parmentier 1987; Sutton 1998) analyze local historical consciousness, though without emphasizing literacy. Other anthropological studies of Latin American literacy include the following: Campbell (1995:157–165); Gebhart-Sayer (1985); Gow (1990); Guevara-Gil and Salomon (1994); Harris (1995); Hill and Wright (1988); Hornberger (ed.) (1997); Howe (1979); Jaye and Mitchell (eds.) (1999); Kalman (1999); Lévi-Strauss (1981:294–300); Orlove (1991); Ortiz Rescaniere (1973); Perrin (1985); Platt (1992); Pollock (1993:185–187); Ramón Valarezo (1991); Sánchez Parga (1983); and Skar (1994).

28. Gruzinski, for example, readily acknowledges this focus:

> Still the nobles of the cities and countryside, the notables of the villages (with or without authentic Titles) do not by themselves stand for indigenous societies and cultures. They make up only a minority sector, perhaps 5 percent (Israel, 1975, p. 44). There remains the enormous mass of population that never had access to the written text, still less to "paintings," those whom we call for the sake of convenience *macehuales,* peasants, artisans, agricultural workers, miners, household staff. [Gruzinski 1993:144–145]

In Gruzinski's study, literacy is essentially the domain of a small group of specialists (albeit the specialists of a subordinate, indigenous group). And though other Latin American studies explore nonspecialist perspectives at greater length, they tend to do so in terms of social memory.

4

God's Book

Not only do the Salasacas believe in a world beyond this one, but they can describe it in vivid detail, based on personal journeys there and reports from friends and relatives who have died and come back to life. The same details appear over and over in these reports: the large, wok-like frying pan under the cemetery where the souls begin their journey, the leaping flames, the black dogs, the hacienda that appears on the path to heaven. In terms of this study, the most interesting aspect of these journeys is that eventually the souls meet God, who has a large book that determines everyone's birth and death date. What are the sources of this book? What might it tell us about Salasaca conceptions of power? And how do these conceptions compare with those contained in the previously discussed witch's book? These are the questions I address in this chapter.

Although I heard various accounts of the other world, the richest one I ever heard was told to me by Julia, the middle-aged mother of the family I lived with in Salasaca (see cover photo and Figure 4.1). It is ironic that Julia's account, based on her detailed recollection of what a man who visited the other world told her several years earlier, is the most elaborate one I heard, because Julia specifically told me several times that she has a poor memory. She made this self-deprecating comment on a few different occasions, though always in a half-joking tone that indicated she didn't really believe it. I never believed it either and told her so, laughing and reminding her of all the detailed childhood memories she had recently recounted. Her response one time was just to laugh and mumble, "I don't know about that," and then look back down at the potatoes she was peeling for that night's dinner. I think she knew I was right, but I could also understand why she might sometimes feel forgetful next to her husband, Alonso. Julia knows that Alonso and I have an intense relationship that revolves around this thing called "anthropology" *(antropología)*, our mutual fascination with Salasaca cultural patterns. But my relatively closer relationship with Alonso has less to do with differences between Alonso and Julia in memory ability than in gender. Alonso is the one who weaves textiles for the market, following the pattern of exclusive male control of weaving since it became commercialized in the wake of government and nongovernmental organization (NGO) programs in the 1960s. Because of my efforts to promote Alonso's weaving sales, I have naturally spent more time talking with him. Also, when I first started visiting their home, Julia was a bit reserved in comparison with Alonso, who took the lead in our conversations. Perhaps Alonso initially felt more comfortable speaking with an obvious outsider like me due to his experience working in construction on the Galápagos Islands as a child; consistent with the village's gender and labor patterns (Poeschel Rees 1985), Julia, on the other hand, has never left Salasaca for an extended period of migratory labor. And perhaps my being male made it initially easier to get close to Alonso, bypassing any of the questions that might accompany a male-female friendship.

But I don't mean to exaggerate these differences. Over the past years, Julia and I have become extremely close, too, especially since when I'm in Salasaca, we live under the same roof. It's hard to be too restrained with someone after you've eaten meals with her day after day, helped care for her young child, and essentially become a part of her family. To this day, some of my fondest memories of my 1994–1995 fieldwork include the nights we would all—Julia, Alonso, their two children, and I— get into bed together, soaking up each other's warmth in the cold Andean evenings while we watched Mexican soap operas on their recently purchased color television. After I'd had my fill of desultory conversation and mass media diversion, I would head off to my room, but even then, I was only a few yards away from them, separated by two wooden walls that didn't reach all the way to the ceiling. Transcribing

Figure 4.1   Julia. Photo by Dennis Pippen.

my interview tapes, I turned up the volume on my headphones to drown out the TV noise, but the illusion that this was anything other than a one-room house was shattered whenever Alonso, Julia, or the kids called to me from their bed, usually with a comment about something they'd just seen on the TV or a question about plans we'd discussed earlier. I was grateful for the privacy they did allow me, but I also came to find these cozy living arrangements deeply fulfilling. If no comments came over the wall at night, I would start to feel lonely and go back to their side for one last chat before the lights were turned out. I once told Julia that, after living with them, I had realized that the U.S. custom of giving babies their own rooms is nothing other than emotional cruelty. When I returned a couple years later, Julia asked if my wife and I still let our baby sleep with us, as I'd vowed to do on my last visit. I was glad to answer yes—and to see once again that Julia's memory is as sharp as anybody's when it comes to topics of interest to her.

Certainly Alonso never discouraged my friendship with his wife or kept her from participating in our conversations. I never detected a hint of jealousy or fears of impropriety from Alonso, or, for that matter, from any other men whose wives I talked with. Of course, it helped that my wife lived with me for part of my fieldwork, and that I didn't usually spend time alone with Salasaca women—or anybody, since various family members were inevitably co-present or working nearby during my visits. Even in these mix-sexed situations, Julia and other Salasaca women showed no trouble speaking their minds.

The day I recorded Julia's story is a good example. Late one afternoon in 1995, I was asking Alonso and Julia for clarification on interviews I recorded earlier that day with other Salasacas. As I took notes, Alonso talked while continuing to weave a belt on the backstrap loom in the house's courtyard. Julia was seated a few feet behind Alonso on a chair improvised from a plastic sack filled with clothes, spinning wool on her distaff with practiced expertise, as if she were simply wiping her fingers together to remove some dust. When I described what I'd just heard about a woman who died and saw God's book, they both confirmed they had heard similar stories and began to add new details. Although Alonso did more of the talking, it was a three-way conversation, as usual. Alonso would start to say something and then ask Julia, "Isn't that right?" Or Julia would simply jump in when she disagreed, remembered other details, or wanted to ask about something Alonso just said. As the conversation circled around, it became clear to me that Salasaca journeys to the other world were not rare, anomalous occurrences, as I first thought, and that Julia was thinking of one special report she'd heard before. I finally asked Julia if I could tape record her report in its entirety, making sure this wasn't a private subject and there wasn't some chore calling her at the moment (we had already repeatedly gone over the issue of my using her words). After Julia agreed, I took a hand-held tape machine out of the small knapsack at my feet, set it up on a wooden chair in front of Julia, and hit the record button. What follows below is an English translation of Julia's Quichua description of the other world, based on what a man named Clemente Moreta told her a few years earlier.[1] I quote the story at length for several reasons—above all, because I think it provides a fascinating commentary on literacy and power, especially the second part, when Clemente meets God. Reproducing such an elaborate report also helps to redress the dearth of consideration of otherworld experiences in the literature on Andean cultures. Finally, I think this story is easier to read than excerpts from disjointed, multiple accounts would be; Julia portrays, in a continuous narrative, one man's maneuvers through the many perilous obstacles strewn in his path. Julia herself got caught up in this story, her pitch high and her tempo quick as she told it.

RETURNING FROM THE DEAD

[Me:] OK.

[Julia:] OK. A deceased man named Clemente told me this story. He said, what's it called, he said . . .

[Alonso:] Tell the whole thing.

[Julia:] OK. Clemente said, "At the cemetery entrance, there's a frying pan with four handles. There's a frying pan right there, under the ground. And there are four dogs there, tied up with an old chain. Black dogs, almost like wolves. Very, very black, like wolves. Like the devil. And one of them—half his body was pure fire, and the other half was totally black." That's what Clemente said he saw. And he said, "Those dogs sitting there, they try to bite the souls passing by, and they almost bit me."

[Me:] So they're the souls of the dead?

[Julia:] Right, the dead souls. And he said, "Those dogs are devil dogs, and they almost bit me." And then he said, "There's a cooking stone there, and on top of it are many, many witches—witches who kill people. They're burning there, just burning. And there are people burning, too, people who died. Just like a guinea pig, they're burning. And at the foot of the fire there are people burning, as a punishment. Lots of white people and others. It's a terrible punishment. They go straight into the fire, where it's boiling. It's payment for their sins. And that's where those witches try to tie you up. They want to make you stay with them down there, to burn with them. They tie you up at your knees. They tie you up with leather, with all kinds of animal skins, and with the thorns of the cochineal plant. And there's *lots* of fire, *lots* of fire, in that frying pan. It's boiling like mad."

[Me:] So this is all under the ground, where the cemetery door is?

[Julia:] Right. It's underground. It's what the people who die see. It's from another life. We can't see it on this side. Clemente said, "I died at seven in the morning, and at five in the afternoon I came back to life. I was dead a whole day."

[Me:] I see.

[Julia:] Then Clemente said, "I got caught in those flames, but I ran over to the side and hid. And I went through this little door. I went to the sky [*cilumun*]. But, as I was going through the door, my shirt got ripped on the metal. I said, 'Oh, damn!' But I got through. And then I saw these white doves coming, flying over these flames high, high up in the air. The doves kept flying higher and higher to escape, but the flames reached all the way up to them, and just roasted them. Shreds of the birds were falling to the ground. Those birds are the souls of babies who have died. Those little white doves are the babies, the ones who were up to three years old when they died. The kids who are over four have to go and pull out the weeds around some white flowers [*huaita*, Q.]. But the fire killed all the doves; it just caught their wings and burned them. This was punishment for not coming out of their mothers easily, for making their mothers suffer." That's what Clemente said. And you know that place where the black people dance near the cemetery, during the Caporales fiesta?

[Me:] Yes.

[Julia:] Clemente said that under that place there's a lake. We can't see it from here, but he saw it. And he saw a hacienda there, too. And there were these women there, just washing and washing clothes. And these men came by with a whip, and kept heading on to Mount Tungurahua, but since Clemente had participated in the Caporales fiesta, he didn't get punished by them. . . . He just kept going, toward Pelileo. He said, "I just went a little further, and I could see everything: the land below me, the people, the flowers, everything. And then I came to this hacienda where they plant white flowers. They were all little kids, working with these little hoes. These were kids older than four. They were all weeding and planting flowers. The kids were just talking and making all kinds of noise. But they were only twelve years old or younger."

He said, "The kids who are thirteen don't go there. They go to another place. God says it's not right for boys who are only fifteen years old to date girls. He only permits boys and girls to walk around together after they're eighteen. So those who did this when they were fifteen get punished, badly punished. Whether they're boys or girls, they get punished. They're suffering. They're burning up, both the boys and girls." Then Clemente said, "The one who was making the kids and everyone work on the hacienda was an old man [*yuyij rucu*]. He's the one who tells them what to do. He's the owner of the hacienda."

[Me:] Was he indigenous?

[Julia:] No. He was white [*chololaya*]. "He had a beard," Clemente said. Uh, huh. Then Clemente said, "I kept going a little further, about another hundred yards, and I came to another hacienda where everyone was working, except this time the workers were old people. They were trying to lift a tree trunk, to use it for firewood. It was just a little trunk, about five feet long, but it was totally rotted out, so they couldn't lift it up. It just kept breaking into pieces. There were about thirty or forty people, but they couldn't raise that trunk. So I asked them, 'What is this?' And they said, 'It's a tree trunk. Please, please could you help us lift it and take it over there?' I said, 'Sure. Just a second.' So I took my poncho off and put it on the ground. And I picked it up really easily, and put it down where they wanted it. But they were scared, just staring at me. They all got together and started chanting at me, 'Raw meat! Raw meat! Raw meat!' That's what all those dead souls were saying."

[Alonso:] Right. They called Clemente "raw meat" because he was still alive, so he hadn't been punished; he hadn't been burned much yet. That's why he could lift the trunk, since he still had his strength. But everybody else was burned meat, maybe except for a nun or someone without sin who could go straight to the sky. But that's rare; everybody has sin.

[Julia:] Right. So Clemente said, "They were screaming 'Raw meat!' and they started hitting me. I could see all these faces, and I knew them all. And then an old man came over and said, 'What are you doing here? Just get out of here. Wherever you were going, just go there. What are you doing here anyway? Just go away.'

"So I left and just started following this path. And then there were two paths: one went this way, and the other went that way. It was a crossroads. One path was beautiful and wide; the other was very narrow, with lots of thorny cochineal plants. So I thought, 'Which one should I take? This one or that one? I know—I'll go this way.' So I started up the clean path, but then I turned around and took the thorny path. Walking and walking, I got really thirsty. But there was no water anywhere, so I just kept going. And along came this dog, a dog who was the color of milk. He didn't have any red, gray, or black, the colors of the devil. It was Little Bear, my dog from this world! And he showed me where to find water, so I could drink, and then he went away."

Clemente said, "And then another door appeared, a big wooden door. And far off in the distance I could see some old man. I went to open the door, but it was closed, so I just waited there, trying to push the door open a little bit. And then this old man with a staff came over. And he asked, 'Why did you come here? Who called you?' I answered, 'I didn't come here without a reason, not in vain. You called me, Master. I didn't come here without a reason, Master. You called me.' Then the old man said, 'Wait here. I'll go get the book.' And the old man went off. He left the door open, but he didn't let me enter the room. I just stood behind the door."

[Me:] Clemente doesn't enter?

[Julia:] Right, he doesn't enter. He doesn't see paradise.

[Me:] Who was that old man?

[Julia:] I don't know. Clemente said he was a very old person. He didn't know him. [I think this "old man" is best seen as a Salasaca version of the Christian God, for reasons explained further below.] So the old man said "Wait, wait here for a minute." Since the old man said that, "I stayed there," Clemente said. "I obeyed," he said, "since the old man had said 'stay.' I didn't enter."

So the old man went to get the book. The book was about this big [with her hands Julia indicates that the book was about a foot in height and width]. Just one book. It was a *very old* book. Then, opening the book, the old man checked the book, sitting there, toward the inside of the room. Clemente was behind him, seeing all this through the doorway. The old man was sitting on some sort of bench, just sitting there. The old man was checking the book, opening the book and looking for Clemente's name. He said, "Wait, I will look for your name. If your name is in the book, you will stay here. If your name is not in the book, you will not stay here; you will go back to earth, returning to your home." "Nobody called you," the old man said [with a tone of irritation]. The old man was checking, reading and reading, reading all the names. All the names, every name.

[Me:] Last names?

[Julia:] Yes. After reading for a while, the old man said, "Your name is not here." Then the old man began looking for the name of Clemente's wife, and that name was there. "Listen," the old man said, "there was no reason for you to come here, but your wife will be coming here in one year, coming to this side. Your wife will come, and she won't go back. She will stay here. Your wife will come here."

Then, once again, the old man started to look for Clemente's name, going through all the names three times. Getting to the end of the names, he started all over again, looking and looking, but he did not find his name. His name wasn't there—not at all, nothing. So the old man said, "No, it's not here. Your name is not here." The old man chided Clemente, saying "Go back! Leave! Why did you come here? I didn't call your name to make you come here. Who called your name to make you come here? Just go back to your home. Your wife is crying, your children are crying; they're very sad, crying and crying there. Why did you come here? Why are you making them cry? Just go back." Clemente said, "But, Master, you yourself called me; that's why I came." But the old man said, "No, I didn't call you. I will call your wife a year later. She will come. But you— just go back to earth."

And, in the middle of the book where Clemente's name should have been, there was an empty line. One line, one empty line. So the old man entered Clemente's name on that line, saying "Your name will remain on this line." Having made the old man write down his name, Clemente came back to life. He said now his name will stay on that line. At that very moment the old man wrote down Clemente's name, but before that it hadn't been there.

[Me:] What else did Clemente get the old man to write down?

[Julia:] It must have been the date on which Clemente was scheduled to die. So then Clemente asked, "Master, when will I die?" The old man said, "Not now. You'll be living this, this, this many more years [while saying this, Julia held up her fingers three times, indicating thirty years]. That's how much longer you'll be living. Just go now." So with the notations done like that, Clemente came back to earth. He wrote with a feather . . .

[Me:] You mean with a pen?[2]

[Julia:] No, he said it was not a pen. It was a chicken's feather that was used to write.

[Me:] Ahhh . . .

[Julia:] Right, a chicken's feather. But he wrote black letters. A white feather, but black ink came out. Like far in the past I've heard they used feathers to write with, like that.

So then "I came back to earth," Clemente said. "I must have come back at that moment, to this side; I just returned," he said. His children, his wife—the children were all crying, the wife, too, just crying terribly. But he came back to life. But then one year later his wife died. His wife did not come back to earth; she just died that way. "She disappeared; she stayed up there," he said. That's exactly the way it was. Maybe when Clemente died the first time he must have been about twenty-four years old, something like that. Yes, something like that. But when he died recently he must have been about seventy-five years old. That's the way he died, a very old man. He was plenty gray by then. Yes, he died, but not getting sick; he was healthy before he died. Maybe he died about three or four years ago, just about that long ago. It's been a while.

◆ ◆ ◆

Thus ended Julia's recapitulation of Clemente's story. After Julia finished, I left the tape recorder on and we all continued talking about the story, Julia, Alonso, and I. Listening to the tape now, some of my clarification questions seem pointless, but at the time I was still trying to wrap my mind around the idea of visiting the other world and living to tell the story, and I wanted to make sure I was hearing correctly. Alonso confirmed that I was, adding a couple other stories he had heard about people who had visited the other world, and over the subsequent months I collected many other accounts, all basically similar to Julia's, though never as elaborate. Some people had only gotten as far as the fires and the lake, though they, too, heard about God's book.

IMAGES OF SURVEILLANCE

As I discovered, Clemente's story contains the basic elements typically found in Salasaca reports about the other world.[3] Other Salasacas repeatedly echoed Clemente's descriptions of the frying pan, the fires, witches, hacienda, and the location of all this on paths starting below the cemetery and leading in the direction of the Amazon.

One man, a farmer, said, "God is waiting at the door. He checks the paper, and says, 'You're not supposed to be here yet. Just go back. After this many years [puts his hands up], you'll be coming back.'" A middle-aged woman said, "There is this big frying pan. And there's lots and lots of fire, just burning people up, especially the witches, the people who did bad things in this life. It's terrible punishment. They really suffer." In fact, many of the same details were also found by Rachel Corr, an anthropologist who carried out in-depth fieldwork in Salasaca and collected similar reports, such as the following:

> In Cruz Pamba there is a *paila* [frying pan or caldron] of flames that the old ones knew about. Right in that crossroads, upon arriving at that crossroads, my grandmother saw black dogs, black dogs, and nobody could pass there. There are black dogs in that *crucero* [crossroads], she said, devils. . . . In that *crucero* she said there are lots of devils, the black dogs are waiting there, the fire caldron is there, with many witches/sorcerers stirring it up, those that practiced witchcraft enter inside the paila, and among themselves they move it, in the *infierno* [Hell]. [Corr 2000:188][4]

For that matter, this imagery is prevalent throughout Latin America, from the symbolism of the fire and thorns to the colors black and white.

As the reference to "Hell" indicates, such imagery is obviously the legacy of Christianization, and not at a superficial level but deeply embedded in the culture, while thoroughly fused with traditional Andean notions of the underworld (e.g., Gelles et al. 1996; Gruzinksi 1993[1988]; MacCormack 1991; Silverblatt 1987). What the Salasacas find on their journeys is entirely consistent with previously published accounts of the Andean other world, though nothing like God's book has been discussed at length before, as far as I know.

At first glance, the most obvious model for God's book is writing associated with haciendas. After all, the man with the book that Clemente meets clearly resembles the hacienda owners he encountered earlier, especially the one who, like the book owner, said, "What are you doing here anyway? Just go away." And Clemente repeatedly refers to the figure with the book as "old man" (yuyij rucito) and "Master" (Taita amo). When I directly asked Julia whether this was God, she said she didn't know, that Clemente only said it was a very old man.[5] So is it even correct to refer to "God's book," as opposed to the book of "the hacienda owner" or "the old man"?

I think it is, for several reasons. In Salasaca, as elsewhere in the Andes, God is seen as a white, male Master or hacienda owner. It's not that heaven is viewed as a place of suffering, like a hacienda: Salasacas say that heaven is a much gentler version of this world, in which everyone plants flowers with their happily reunited family and friends. Nonetheless, as a powerful ruler and the owner of the land, God is similar to a hacienda owner. Catherine Allen's characterization of the Catholic God applies well here: "Imposed on a traumatized population after the Spanish conquest, the Catholic God, modeled on the Hispanic patrón, epitomizes Hispanic domination" (1988:52).[6] It's not surprising, then, that hacienda overtones enter the Salasaca conception of God. Uncertainty also surrounds references to God because he is a remote figure, the last one encountered on journeys through the other world. In fact, Clemente was somewhat unusual in making it all the way to God's door; many others only report arriving at the earlier points, such as the frying pan or the haciendas. Hacienda overtones and uncertainty notwithstanding, it's significant that Clemente explicitly states, "I went to the sky [cilumun]." For the Salasacas, God resides in the sky: hence the Quichua term for "heaven" is *cilu,* from the Spanish word for "sky" *(cielo).*[7] And virtually everyone I spoke to about this book explicitly referred to it as the possession of "God" *(Taita Dios).* Though some people alternated "God" with "Master" *(Taita amo),* when I directly asked about the man's identity, they said it was God himself *(Dioslladij).* I think it makes sense, then, to refer to the figure in these stories as God.

Moreover, no Salasaca ever readily compared God's book with hacienda papers. They consistently compared it, instead, with birth certificates and baptism books, as in the following statements:

> 1) *God is in an office, and he has your name written down, like in a baptism book. He writes your name down when you're born. He runs things like the government, like the Civil Registry—exactly like that.*
>
> 2) *We have our names registered at the Civil Registry, right? God has it all exactly like that.* (Shutida asentachinchi, na chu? Shinaidij Dios charin).
>
> 3) *My godmother* [who died and came back] *said that the dead souls go to this nice room, like the Civil Registry office.*
>
> 4) *My friend said, "Just like at the Civil Registry we have them search for our birth certificate* [imalaya Registro Civilbi ñucuchij partida mashcachinchi], *exactly like that we have our names searched. If the name isn't there, you come back to life. Our names are there, like in the church. That's what's there, in heaven* [jahua cilubi]."

Such comparisons were repeatedly made between God's book and church and state documents, especially baptism books and Civil Registry birth certificates. Significantly, not only did some Salasacas mention that God is in an office (that is, like a priest or bureaucrat, not a hacienda owner), but everyone said God writes your name and death date in his book when you're born: "He writes it down after the child is born"; "God writes your name down when you're born." God's book therefore consists of names, with birth and death dates, exactly like baptism books and birth certificates, as well as funeral and death certificates. This correspondence also makes sense in terms of Salasaca history (described in earlier chapters). The church and Civil Registry have for centuries played a large role in Salasaca experiences, whereas the Salasacas never became absorbed into an hacienda.

God's book even resembles Jorge Luis Borges' vision of the "Library": "But the certainty that everything has been already written nullifies or makes phantoms of us all. . . . Perhaps I am deceived by old age and fear, but I suspect that the human species—the unique human species—is on the road to extinction, while the Library will last on forever: illuminated, solitary, infinite, perfectly immovable, filled with precious volumes, useless, incorruptible, secret" (Borges 1962:87). God's book is nothing if not an image of universal, powerful, permanent, and comprehensive knowledge. The Salasacas exhibit their sense of God's omniscience every time they say *jahua pacha,* meaning "By God, it's true." The idea is that something was witnessed by God from above *(jahua),* so it absolutely must have happened. With this same omniscience, God enters everybody's name in his book, almost always at birth but sometimes later, when someone like Clemente arrives in heaven ahead of schedule. Since the Salasacas see archival writings as instruments of surveillance that define individual existence, they logically assume that God, the supreme source of control, has an extremely powerful book, one that determines when individuals will be born and when they will die.[8]

More specifically, God's book represents strict order. Everyone's name gets entered in his book on a separate line, and everyone is supposed to arrive in heaven or hell according to an exact date written in the book. Thus, the minute details of graphic organization reveal fundamental processes of social control. The key term here is *hila,* which has a revealing range of uses. *Hila* is the Quichua pronunciation of the Spanish word *fila,* meaning "row," "line," or "queue."[9] *Hila* can refer not only to "lined paper" *(hila rurashca papil),* but also a queue of people *(hilabi shayarin).* With the locative suffix *bi* added, the term *hilabi* carries a sense of order, of things being done properly according to proscribed rules. These various meanings come together in God's book.

The Salasacas say God's book must be written on lined paper, echoing their conception of San Gonzalo's book and reflecting their previous literacy experiences. Most of the writings Salasacas have encountered in the past century, including birth certificates and legal documents, have consisted of lined paper, usually a type with numbers for each line known as *hila rurashca papil,* literally, "paper made with lines/rows." The lines on the paper also determine the order in which people are born or die. Reading God's book, you would see the exact progression of all births and deaths in the world: the next line down contains the name of the next person to be born or to die. God's book therefore represents extreme orderliness. Birth and death are all part of God's master plan—a strict, written plan. This makes it easy for Salasacas to move from talking about God's book to talking about death as something that happens "in order" *(hilabi).* As one man said, "Just as they write down a baptized child's name in order, that's the way we arrive in God's land; we have to arrive in order" *(hilabi chayana gan).* Another man said, "I've heard that we all have to come to God when we're called, in order." And others talked about birth in the same way, as something that happens *hilabi.* The lines in God's book are consistent, in other words, with an ordered universe in which events occur according to plan.

Furthermore, queues—lines of bodies—have been an important part of the Salasacas' experiences with major Hispanic institutions, including schools, the church, and army. Throughout primary and secondary education, the Salasacas are exposed to linear ordering through the rituals of attendance-taking. At the start of the school day and after recess, teachers take attendance by reading off class lists and organizing students in lines. The term *fila* is constantly used, as teachers instruct students to be quiet, well mannered, and to make good, orderly rows *(¡Hay que hacer filas! ¡Buena fila!).* Such queuing is referred to in Spanish as "formation" *(formación),* which also means "training" or "upbringing." Several meanings of lines are thus melded together and drilled into young Salasacas during these daily rituals: lines on the paper; lines of people; the importance of lines for control and socialization. Such queues are an obvious example of regimentation, a way of instilling a sense of linear order in the Salasacas' body memory. Not surprisingly, Salasacas carry this sense over to their image of God's book, explicitly comparing school attendance taking and God's calling of names. As one woman said, "When we die, God calls our name, reading off his list. They call off all the names at school, right? Well, it's just like that in God's land." Another said, "He has a list with names, like Virgilio or Manuel. He calls your name and then says 'Come.' He's reading and calling at the same time, like a school list."

Emphasis on line formation is pervasive in other domains as well. Although the Salasacas have avoided military service until recently because of exemptions for indigenous groups, they are well aware that ordered lines are a central part of army training. As one young man put it, "I heard that's all they do: just make you march around all day." Military-style marching also pervades civic parades carried out by local whites. In fact, the Spanish word for "parade," *desfile*, derives from the verb *desfilar*, which means "to march or walk in line" and derives from the same word for "line" *(fila)*. Finally, the church uses lines for virtually all its rituals, not only inside the church, but also entering and exiting the church and in processions through the central plaza. Thus, line formation is clearly connected with three major white institutions: the church, army, and school. When these queues are combined with the lines in church and state documentation, it's easy to understand why the Salasacas also use the word *hila* to denote order and describe God's book.[10]

The special meaning of *hila* is further highlighted by contrasting it with two other lines: rows in farms and lines in woven belts. Both of the latter are pervasive aspects of daily, adult Salasaca experience, which should make them likely source domains for metaphors of order, yet they do not take on such extended meanings the way *hila* does. Neatly spaced-out rows of crops present an obvious model of straight lines, and, given the importance of farming, the term for such rows, *huachu*, is frequently used in Salasaca speech. Nevertheless, *huachu*, unlike *hila*, is not used to mean orderliness. *Llanu*, another potential metaphor source, describes the row of straight, vertical lines found at the ends of the woven belts worn daily by Salasaca women, yet *llanu* lines are not used as images of order. *Hilabi*, by contrast, evokes a specific type of order associated with powerful, non-indigenous institutions.[11] God's book derives, in short, from specific textual models, notably baptism books and birth certificates, as well as a general association between lines, power, and control.

COMMENTARY ON POWER AND GENDER

The Salasaca attitude toward God's book is one of acceptance. There is no protest to be made against God, a strict, supreme authority, or his book, with its comprehensive, linear record of every person on earth. Deaths recorded in God's book occur as inevitably as the movement of the eye down the page, from one line to the next. No Salasaca, in fact, ever reported bargaining with God, not even Clemente. Of course Clemente had no reason to ask God not to send him back to earth, but presumably he wanted to protest God's decree that his wife would die one year later. Nonetheless, Clemente doesn't even think to ask God to alter his decision, to scratch out his wife's death date and enter a later one for her, or a later death date for himself, for that matter. Granted, there is a trickster-like element to Clemente's journey, as he dodges the perilous traps in his path. In the end, though, whatever happened to Clemente, whether he made it to heaven or got snared in the fires, would have been God's decision. Death dates, in particular, cannot be altered, even in the cases where a bookkeeping mistake has occurred. In his meeting with God, the closest Clemente comes to protesting is to point out that God himself had called him there, yet this only answers God's question about who called him, and it simply refers to an earlier command from God. Genuine protest is beyond the question. What could any human possibly offer God or say to make him change his plans? Nothing, according to the Salasacas, who are otherwise adept in evading the clutches of extreme power. Alonso and Julia said it wouldn't have done Clemente any good to argue with God, and others similarly dismissed this option.

This power is so systematic that the Salasacas found it strange when I asked if God's death dates are fair. Taken aback for a moment, most answered yes, or, uncomfortable with the idea of second-guessing God, said something like, "That's just the way it is." Several used the same phrase: "That's what God commands" (*Taita Dios shina mandan*). I asked this question because I could think of several potential reasons to resent God's rulings. First, God's gruff manner resembles the impoliteness of state bureaucrats dealing with Indians. God could also be criticized as a strict male authority figure, one who has even usurped female reproductivity by deciding when babies are born. God's authoritarianism contrasts not only with the Salasacas' more consensual approach to community decision making, but also the relative egalitarianism in their gender relations, largely due to female land ownership and the important role of women in agricultural production, as documented throughout the Andes (Allen 1988; Belote and Belote 1988; Borque and Warren

1981; Corr 2002:17; Hamilton 1998; Harris 1978; Isbell 1978; Poeschel Rees 1985). Alonso and Julia's relationship, for example, seems to be based on mutual devotion, respect, and cooperation. I was always touched to hear them in the next room talking together at night for hours on end against the TV's din, ruminating in minute detail over a conversation one of them had earlier that day with a friend, or formulating decisions about new purchases or other plans. And these moments were not just limited to late-night conversations. When Julia told me Clemente's story, Alonso listened raptly, without trying to steal the floor or displaying jealousy. Though Alonso went on to amplify certain points with details he had heard elsewhere, he had no trouble admitting that he'd never heard this particular report before (as Julia pointed out, he was raised in a different part of the village, so he never knew Clemente). I don't mean to idealize Andean gender relations—there were certainly times when Alonso took the lead, and it's difficult to say that Andean social relations are perfectly complementary (Arnold [ed.] 1997). Still, a degree of gender egalitarianism prevails in Salasaca, so I thought a contrast could be made with God's authoritarianism, yet neither Alonso, Julia, nor any other Salasaca ever saw this as noteworthy. After nearly five centuries of exposure and accommodation to Hispanic society (Silverblatt 1987), male rule did not strike them as odd, especially in God, the supreme white authority. "That's just the way God is," Julia said.

Acceptance is not, however, the Salasacas' final response. In the next chapter we'll find that the Salasacas have actively sought to appropriate writing's power. If the analysis stopped at God's book, we would be left with an incomplete picture of Salasaca culture.

Notes

1. Of course, translating across two languages is not straightforward. A question arises here, for example, about how to translate the evidential markers embedded in Julia's Quichua speech. Not only did Clemente report to Julia his talk with God, but Julia is now narrating Clemente's report to me. Since Quichua requires distinctions about the source for a given stretch of discourse (whether the events were observed first hand or not), Julia uses reported speech verbs ("he said") and the evidential

marker *shca* throughout her account. For the sake of readability, however, I omit most of these quotation markers in my English translation. Given the layers of reported speech at the end of the account, in particular (where I'm quoting Julia quoting Clemente quoting God), I mix in more of a third-person perspective. I have also omitted some of my clarification questions, since they did not significantly affect the narration: once in motion, Julia did not need prompts of any sort to keep the story moving. As these decisions indicate, I try to strike a balance between fidelity to the Quichua original and English readability, a translation approach close to that of Paul Gelles and Gabriela Martínez Escobar: "Again, our main goal has been to provide a text that flows and communicates in English the ease and naturalness with which the narrators imparted their lives to their interlocutors. In sum, the text effects a compromise between a strict ethnopoetic standard and a relatively 'free' translation" (1996:6). For excellent discussions of issues raised in translating from Quichua to English, see Gelles et al. (1996); Harrison (1989); Mannheim (1991); and Salomon and Urioste (1991).

2. I ask this question because the Salasacas, like most Ecuadorians, do not normally use the Spanish word "feather" *(pluma)* for "pen": instead, they prefer the terms *esfero* (Ecuadorian Sp.) or *boli,* a shortened form of the Spanish word *bolígrafo.* On the other hand, feather pens were obviously used in the past, as Julia recognizes and as is reflected in some Salasaca elders' use of the term "to scratch" *(aspina)* to mean "to write," rather than the more common *escribina.*

3. It would have been just as easy to call this Julia's story, since she has retold Clemente's story according to her own interpretation. The less typical aspects of Clemente's story are noted below.

4. See Corr (2000:182–216) for an excellent discussion of Salasaca reports about the other world. Corr (2000:189) translates *paila* as "caldron" rather than "frying pan" because some Salasacas report that the souls are boiling, and because of European imagery that Corr perceptively traces back to seventeenth-century European paintings and local church iconography. In fact, Julia and others also mention that the fire boils *(timbun)* the souls; and the pan they describe is so deep it could certainly be referred to as a caldron as well. I have chosen to use the term "wok-like frying pan" in keeping with the more common sense of *paila* (which Corr

also notes) and because some Salasacas explicitly compare the under-world *paila* with pans used to make french fries. Although her accounts do not include mention of "raw meat," Corr (2000:77) mentions another story, like Clemente's, about dead people who can't pick up a plant and who don't like the smell of a live soul's farts, literally, "raw breath" *(chahua sami)*.

5. Clemente uses several variations on these terms, including *yuyij rucito, yuyij rucu, rucito yuyij,* and *rucu* for "old man," and *Taita amo, Taita amito, Taita,* and *Patrón* for "Master." Each of these terms is used one to two times by Clemente in this section of his text.

6. Allen (1988:52) also points out that this Christian God is similar to the Incan sun deity, who was remote and associated with the Inca nobility. See also Isbell (1978:151), Lyons (1998:40), and Rasnake (1988a:236) for other examples of Andean male deities envisioned as white men, fused with mountain spirits.

7. Other terms for heaven are "the upper world" *(jahua pacha)* and "God's land" *(Diosbug llacta)*.

8. Other possible sources for God's book are "morality ledgers." For exam-ple, Donald Joralemon and Douglas Sharon, in their discussion of Peruvian shamanism, refer to the Book of Life and Satan's records (1993:280, note 5). Although these books share interesting features with God's book, it is not clear they are related in Salasaca. Like most Latin American peasants, the Salasacas believe in devil pacts, one of the legacies of colonialism (Silverblatt 1987), yet they do not speak of a book owned by Satan. Instead, their devil pacts are formed through dreams of the devil, sex with the devil, or a witch's rituals. The Salasacas are also well aware of the notion of Judgment Day *(Juicio P'unlla)*, but I only found one person who had heard that God will use a book to separate the sin-ners from the true believers. Of course it's possible that historically no-tions of God's book were influenced by (Salasaca interpretations of) church teachings about Judgment Day, but I have no way to prove this one way or the other. Undoubtedly, notions of morality ledgers are preva-lent elsewhere in Latin America. Ruth Behar, for example, notes that "The idea of spiritual accounting is a constant theme in Mexican women's pop-ular discourse" (1993:356, note 13). For that matter, similar metaphors are found in North America (Lakoff 1995:178–180).

9. Younger Salasacas sometimes simply say *filabi* rather than *hilabi*.

10. This is not to imply that lines are only used by external sources of institutional control. The Salasacas themselves now use written attendance lists to charge fines for late arrival at meetings, such as meetings for irrigation groups.

11. Other common words for paper lines are *linea* and *raya* (both from Spanish), but older people still sometimes use the word *aspinaguna*, i.e., "the scratchings." It may be that the use of the term "scratchings" derives from earlier use of chicken feathers for pens, a term that might imply a vision of writing as more erratic and less controlled (cf. Messick 1989:46). One old person also told me that his grandmother referred to the lines in paper as *huachu* (field row). Though they are suggestive, it is hard to know how widely these other terms were used in the past.

5

The Day of the Dead

During the Day of the Dead ceremonies in November, the Salasacas attend Mass to hear a priest read off lists with the names of each family's deceased relatives. Afterward, the priest is supposed to hand the lists back to their respective owners, who later stash the lists in a secret place in their homes. The Mass I observed in 1994, however, involved a breakdown in the usual pattern. This priest, having recently arrived from another province and not knowing the Salasacas' customs, simply walked off and left the lists sitting in a pile on the altar. At first nobody was sure what to do, but soon dozens of Salasacas emptied the pews and descended on the altar to look for their lists. Chaos ensued, since only a few people could see the lists and not all could read them, at least not quickly enough for the frantic crowd pressed in around them. As people clamored for their lists, the original pile fissioned into several smaller ones, and the noise level continued to rise, along with the frustrations of those who had not yet found their lists. The priest must have heard this commotion, because he suddenly reemerged from behind the altar and yelled at the Salasacas for making so much noise. Saying they had to leave immediately, he shooed everyone down the aisle and out of the church. On the church steps outside, some people dropped the remaining sheets to the ground, allowing them to get caught in gales of wind and take flight. One of my saddest memories is the sight of elderly Salasacas grabbing at passing lists, sometimes on the verge of tears, as if the vanishing lists were their own escaping spiritual essence. After more scrambling in vain, no-body was left on the steps except for a few people reconciling themselves to the loss of their lists, whether to a fellow Salasaca or the wind.

This scene made it clear to me that these little pieces of paper were deeply important to the Salasacas, but I wasn't sure why. The most obvious possibility was fear of witchcraft, especially in light of beliefs about San Gonzalo; and, indeed, a few Salasacas expressed fear that enemies could do them harm if they got a hold of their list of souls. However, witchcraft turned out not to be the main factor in this case. The ones who raised the possibility of witchcraft (in response to my hypothetical questions) were those who write their own names at the top of the list, but most Salasacas do not do this, so, as some pointed out, they couldn't be vulnerable to witchcraft; the list only contains the names of the dead, who can't be killed or harmed through witchcraft. The practice of retaining the old lists in the house is also incomprehensible from the perspective of witchcraft. If Salasacas were afraid that the lists could be used for witchcraft, they would burn or otherwise dispose of them after the Day of the Dead, as people do when they get their name removed from San Gonzalo's book; instead, they retain a pile of these lists for years in their homes. Fear of witchcraft, then, did not motivate Salasacas to retrieve their lists of souls on the church steps that day in 1994, and it certainly does not motivate the Salasacas to save the lists in their house year after year.[1]

So I kept wondering: Why do Salasacas retrieve these lists every year after the Mass and store them in their homes? In this chapter, I answer this question by exploring the way these lists appropriate church and state power, and I end by putting all the magical lists in comparative perspective.

COOLING OFF THE DEAD SOULS

The Day of the Dead is a syncretic mixture of pre-Hispanic cosmology and Catholicism, representing the confluence of the traditional cult of the dead and All Souls' Day on November 2. This is the time when the souls of the Salasacas' ancestors return en masse, hungry, thirsty, and agi-tated, and the living endeavor to send them back to the other world by remembering, feeding, thanking, cleansing, and appeasing them.[2] The singular term "Day of the Dead" is actually a misnomer, because this ritual complex spans numerous days and even months. Many souls announce their return by appearing before November with increasing frequency in the dreams of the living, considered real encounters with the dead souls. Even without promptings from dreams, everyone has to begin their preparations in the months before November, laying aside food and assembling a presentable outfit, often buying or weaving and dyeing new clothes. The main rituals finally begin on the evening of November 1 *(Finas Tuta)*, when bread, fruit, and other foods and drinks are laid out for each household's dead souls, with directions to come and eat: "Eat, Grandma; this is for you; eat, Uncle Juan; this is for you." (Although the food and drink remain untouched, their flavor is enjoyed by the souls.) Then on November 2, the "Big Day" *(Jatun P'unlla)*, every family goes to the cemetery and sits together on the grave site of its recently deceased relatives. Cloths are spread out and food shared in a moveable feast of guinea pig, rabbit, potatoes, bread, gruel, assorted fruits, and alcohol.

These first ritual phases will be familiar to readers exposed to images of the Mexican Day of the Dead, but my interest here is in what happens the next day, when the Salasacas have their name lists read during the special Mass for the dead known as the Response Mass *(misa de Responso,* Sp.).[3] The name lists are crucial to the Salasacas because they "cool off" the dead souls. When people leave for the Mass, they commonly say "Come on, let's go cool off the souls" *(Hakuchi, almagunada chiriyachingabug)* or they make a similar reference to "cooling." These are references to the hot-cold classification system found throughout Latin America, a system historically based on Greek humoral theory (Foster 1953, 1994) and arguably spliced onto indigenous notions of duality (Bastien 1985, 1989; López Austin 1980). Because of its flexibility, simplicity, and comprehensiveness, the hot-cold system has proved remarkably tenacious. Virtually any illness can be placed in a binary category of hot or cold, and treatments, determined largely through trial and error, follow the principle that opposites cure. The dead souls do not suffer from such ailments, but they are burning up with hunger, thirst, sadness, and agitation—states of disequilibrium classified as hot for both the living and the dead. In addition, the souls have just returned from the other world, a place of frying pans, tall flames, and extreme heat. Since virtually all dead souls burn for their sins, the living are obliged to cool them off by having the list of souls sprinkled with holy water at the Response Mass.

After the main service, someone from each family approaches the altar, makes a small donation, and hands the list of souls to the priest (or sacristan), who reads the names off the list and sprinkles it with holy water. According to the Salasacas, the dead souls are present at that moment in the list, and they get cooled off by the holy water. One man said, "When the priest throws the holy water [on the list], I say to myself, 'I'm cooling off the dead souls.'" When I attended another Response Mass in 1995, the sacristan, a young Salasaca man, tried to skip sprinkling the holy water on one list because the crowds were so overwhelming. The skipped list owner wouldn't hear of this; he told the sacristan to add the holy water "so as to cool off the souls." A few Salasacas, unsatisfied with just one sprinkle, even asked for a second measure on their lists. After the sacristan finished his duties, I asked him why everyone wanted holy water so much; he said they tell him it's to cool off the dead souls.[4]

Holy water has a cooling effect because it is a major symbol of the church's blessing—from baptisms and funerals to blessings of abandoned houses—and it offers protection from the devil, an extremely hot force from the fires below. The list functions like *chicha*, a traditional Andean corn beer that Salasacas drink in nearby taverns after the Response Mass. This drinking, which lasts into the night or later, is unanimously agreed to cool off the dead souls, as is the pouring of chicha on the ancestors' grave sites the previous day. Chicha is also physically cold—its temperature drops after fermenting in earthen tunnels—and it is symbolically equated with holy water in other death rituals (discussed below), during which Salasaca men imitate priests by sprinkling chicha on ritual attendees while stating "This is holy water" *(Caiga agua benditami gan)*. Chicha, holy water, and written names are therefore crucial elements for cooling off the dead souls.[5]

APPROPRIATING CHURCH POWER

What I've said so far explains why the lists are created before going into the church, but why is it so important to save them once Mass is over? I initially thought the answer was simple: the lists are used to remember the names of the ancestors. That was, in fact, precisely what the Salasacas told me when I initially asked. Everyone mentioned something about remembering the souls' names, often using the phrase "so as not to forget the names" *(ama cungaringabug shutigunada)*. For quite awhile I assumed this meant that the same lists were reused year after year or scribes recopied new lists from previous ones. Later, however, I was forced to reevaluate my assumption.

After the Day of the Dead in 1994, I spent time talking about but rarely seeing the Salasacas' lists of souls, since they are stored in the house in a secret place, usually wrapped in a cloth and stuffed in the roof rafters or a wood chest. Sensing that people were reluctant to take their lists out of their hiding places, I didn't push the issue, nor did I feel the need to, since some families had already shown me their lists and everyone else didn't mind describing theirs in detail. Nonetheless, when the Response day rolled around again in 1995, I wanted to observe the lists as closely as possible, to see if I'd missed anything. Arriving at the church before the eleven A.M. Response Mass, I watched many lists being written by non-Salasaca scribes, two white boys about thirteen years old who showed up on the church steps with notebooks and ballpoint pens in hand. After writing down names on a page in his notebook, each boy ripped out the page, gave it to his Salasaca client, and in return received 500 sucres (approximately 50 cents).[6] I still wanted an even closer look at the lists, but I didn't feel comfortable looking directly over the boys' shoulders, so I decided to become a list scribe myself. Taking a pen and notebook out of my small knapsack, I set myself up on the other side of the steps and yelled out in Quichua, "I'll make your lists for free!" Within a few moments Salasacas were crowding around me, ready to take me up on my offer, and I proceeded to write out about twenty five lists. This struck me as a fair arrangement: some Salasacas got lists for free that year; the boys were still hired by the many Salasacas who couldn't wait for me before Mass started; and I saw more lists in under an hour than I'd seen the entire previous year. After seeing all these lists, I realized something important: the lists are composed from oral memory. Virtually everyone dictated a new list from memory, rattling off the names of their ancestors without consulting any papers or asking to have an old list recopied.[7] The list was not being used as a mnemonic device, after all.

In retrospect, I should have suspected that the lists depend on oral memory when I realized how few names they contain. As I'd heard previously and confirmed that day, the lists only include an average of ten to fifteen names, depending on the number of dead relatives. One man's list, for example, stretched back only to his grandparents and didn't include his wife's relatives, since the wife's parents were still living and had created their own list:

List of Souls (*Lista De Almas*)
Father's father
Father's mother
Father
Sister
Brother
Mother's father
Mother's mother
Mother

Even the longer lists didn't stretch back further than the great-grandparents' generation. Indeed, many people said they only put down names of relatives they had known personally.[8] These processes of forgetting, of cutting off the names at a definite point, explain why the lists haven't grown fantastically long over time.

I knew all this, but I had been thrown off by the Salasacas' explicit statements about using the lists to remember names, statements I was disinclined to question because they fit well with my own sense of writing as a mnemonic device, which the Salasacas seemed to share, at least in the case of God's and San Gonzalo's books. I also assumed the lists helped recall hard-to-remember names (such as great-grandparents'), and that when Salasacas said they had lists made (*listada rurachinchi*), they meant they had scribes or others recopy previous lists. Having been corrected that day, I went back afterward to ask more about the lists' composition. Everyone confirmed that they made up a new list every year. Even in the cases where the list was made up at home rather than on the church steps, they said the lists were dictated from memory rather than being recopied from previous lists; the eldest members of the family recalled the names while a younger, literate member wrote them down. I could have asked why they hadn't told me this before, but I figured the rightful answer would have been "You never asked." People had also understandably been less eager to talk about processes of forgetting than of remembering the dead souls. I asked, though, why they said the list helped recall the names if, in practice, it wasn't used that way. One man answered, "But we need the list, just in case . . ." Others also still maintained that the lists are needed to remember the names, often using the same phrase, "just in case . . . " *(de repente)*.

Eventually I realized that the expression "just in case" is the key to the lists' meaning. "Just in case" perfectly captures the function of an archive: namely, to preserve written documents for those rare moments when they might be consulted in the future. The list of souls represents, once again, the Salasacas' grasp of archival writing. Like San Gonzalo's and God's books, the lists constitute archives: they get collected together, wrapped in cloth (a type of book binding), and safely stored for long periods of time, to be rarely (if ever) consulted at future dates.

And, in each case, these archived, black, written names become individual souls. But whereas the other two archives cause or prevent death, the list of souls is used to remember deceased relatives—or, rather, to prove that such remembrance has taken place.[9] From beginning to end of this ritual complex, the Salasacas are remembering the dead, and the list of souls officially confirms this. The list resembles other church and state documents in verifying that a ritual occurred.[10] The list enjoys the hallmarks of ritual authority, since it is written with black ink on lined paper and a priest (or sacristan) reads and sprinkles the official-register names (never Quichua abbreviations or nicknames) with holy water. The list is therefore stored in the house as tangible, authoritative proof that the dead souls were properly honored.

There is an even more fundamental, underlying reason to save the lists: it allows each Salasaca household to appropriate religious control over relations with the dead. The lists imitate church archives through their contact with holy water, priests, the church, and the Mass, as well as their systematic storage in each home. Each Salasaca household transforms itself into a church by controlling two major symbols of religious authority: archived name lists and holy water. For almost five centuries, writing and holy water have been highly visible aspects of church authority in baptisms, marriages, funerals, and other ritual contexts: being sprinkled with holy water and registered in archives is what moves individuals across the threshold from pagan to Christian in the baptism ritual, and into states of marriage and death in other major sacraments. Salasacas understandably want to snatch some of this power for themselves, especially for the purpose of remembering and honoring the dead souls, the most important ritual charge undertaken annually by every family.

PATTERNS OF APPROPRIATION

Such appropriation of church symbols fits a pattern prevalent in Salasaca and other parts of the Andes. To take one major example, the Catholic Eucharist is imitated with "bread babies" (*tanda huahuaguna*; see Figure 5.1), a traditional food consumed during the Day of the Dead. In preparation for the rituals commencing in November, Salasacas buy small rolls or bake their own at the homes of those who own earthen ovens. Alonso's mother has one such oven, so I spent two days at her house in the last week of October, greeting the stream of neighbors and relatives who showed up with large plastic sacks of flour, ready to bake bread. Aside from bringing over firewood to stoke the oven, I wasn't much help: I spent most of my time sharing bread and stories with the visitors, and making bread figures with Alonso's son, Holguer, and the other children. It was like a cross between Christmas and Thanksgiving for the children: they had all the bread they could eat, lots of family and friends around, and plenty of games to play with the figures of humans and animals fashioned out of flour and baked in the oven. While the children played, the adults baked piles of small, white rolls. Eventually everyone hauled away their rolls in the flour sacks, rolls that would be consumed during the Day of the Dead and afterward. The term "bread baby" refers not only to these white rolls and children's zoomorphic breads but especially to certain anthropomorphic breads bought in nearby stores, with facial features and other sugary, food-colored designs that the Salasacas say they can't create on their own.[11]

These breads represent the children who have died in each family—hence the number and sex of the breads match those of the family's dead children—and they get named as such when food is laid out for the returning souls on the eve of the Big Day. Just as the living like to play with and eat bread babies, the dead children are said to do the same with these store-bought breads, so, along with other favorite foods, the bread babies get carried to the cemetery on the Big Day. But whereas *chicha* (corn beer) is poured out on the grave sites and other foods (including the un-

Figure 5.1   "Bread babies" consumed during the Day of the Dead. This bread depicts a mother holding her baby. Photo by Dennis Pippen.

named white rolls) are eaten by the living to feed the dead, at the end of the day the bread babies remain uneaten, and get brought back to the house and tucked away in a cloth. Several months or a year later, the family takes out this bread (which is rock hard by now), breaks it into pieces, and eats it. Bread babies thus resemble the Catholic Eucharist: someone dies, turns into bread, and later gets eaten. The bread baby is the counterpart to the list of souls, the bread representing deceased small children and the list containing the names of the adult family members who have died. It is fitting, then, that the lists and bread babies usually get stored together, whether in the same trunk or section of the roof rafters (albeit in separate cloths); they belong together as representations of the dead that follow the doctrine of transubstantiation.

Given the bread babies' roots in Catholic and pre-Hispanic rituals, it is not surprising to find them similarly consumed in other parts of the Andes. Joanne Rappaport (1998[1990]) describes the Nasa of Colombia baptizing baby bread and dipping the pieces into corn beer. Mary Weismantel has argued that the Eucharist infuses the meaning not just of Andean bread babies but also a red-black colored gruel *(yana api)*, another required Day of the Dead food in Ecuador and Peru: "These paired symbolic foods, bread in human form and a dark liquid, evoke the symbolism of the Catholic Mass: the Body and Blood of Christ, an image further reinforced by the spoken rituals of the day, when the Mass or fragments of it are recited in the name of the dead" (1991:868). Weismantel traces bread consumption back to Inca rituals, including the Feast of the Sun and Citua, another major feast day and the only other time of the year when the Inca ate bread. In the latter festival, bread was mixed with human blood, leading Weismantel to conclude that "The pairing of blood and bread in the Andes, then, stands for both communion and sacrifice, but it has other roots besides the Catholic Mass" (1991:872; see also Corr 2002:19).*

Salasacas similarly imitate the Catholic Church during another death ritual: the "Head Mass" (Mundungu Misa), a funeral ritual that offers a revealing parallel to the Day of the Dead. The Head Mass occurs at the home of the deceased's family, following the wake, church Mass, and the coffin's burial in the cemetery. Late in the afternoon, when guests are thoroughly inebriated, the Mass is officiated by two Salasaca men who imitate priests by draping woven belts over their shoulders. The humor in this role reversal isn't lost on anybody, especially since an equivalence is implied between the woven belts, obvious markers of Indianness, and vestments, symbols of the priests' authority on the altar. Another Salasaca man often acts as the sacristan, taking a child's notebook or other papers out of the house and pretending to note down names. With this ritual paraphernalia, the "Salasaca priests" then say prayers for the dead, such as Our Father and the Ave Maria, and use a branch to sprinkle those present with corn beer, saying "This is holy water." Rachel Corr, who has done extensive research in Salasaca, adds that the "priests hand out raw potato slices, which they call the body of Christ. . . . The Andean potato, as a metaphor for the Eucharist, is employed in this ritual of death to send the soul off to its new life" (2002:14).

This funeral ritual clearly parodies a Catholic Mass. But while humorous, this indigenous Mass does serious work by sending the de-

---

* Writing about Bolivia, Thomas Abercrombie (1998:364) describes corn beer used to imitate communion wine, and Joseph Bastien (1978:185) describes an indigenous funeral Mass, where baby breads are baptized and an indigenous "priest" says, "This is my dead baby; eat him." As Bastien explains, "The second part of the Feast with the Dead refers to the Catholic rituals of baptism, mass, and communion, which is a parody of birth, death, and eating of the Eucharist" (ibid.).

ceased's soul off to the other world. The Head Mass was variously described to me as the time when "we send the souls to the sky," "we say good-bye to the souls," "we make the souls fly away," and "we make the souls get lost." Before the Head Mass, I heard the deceased person still referred to in the present tense as someone who "dies" *(huañun)*; only after the Head Mass (and the house purification that followed) was the soul referred to in the past tense, as a member of the other world. Thus, the Salasacas, *not* the priests, bid the final farewell to the dead in this ritual, just as they do during the Day of the Dead.[12]

During the final phase of both rituals, dead souls are sent off to the other world, and Salasacas appropriate church symbols to realize this effect. Like holy water, bread babies, black gruel, and potato slices, the list of souls allows Salasacas to adopt church symbols to appease, honor, and remember the dead and thereby send them back to the other world for another year. And that's why, I finally realized, the list of souls gets retrieved after the Response Mass ends.

But is it correct to call this an "appropriation" of church power? Catholic and indigenous cultural elements are so thoroughly mixed together in the Day of the Dead, as in most other Andean rituals, that it may not even make sense to speak of appropriation, with its implication of two distinct cultural realms. We can, nonetheless, recognize the culturally salient difference between public and private ritual spheres; the Salasacas' hiding the lists of souls in their houses clearly belongs to the latter. Archival writing and holy water, on the other hand, have for centuries been exclusively controlled by the church in public rituals—which is why the Salasacas think it's so funny to see one of their own men, equipped with chicha and papers he can't read, say Mass like a priest. The church has also traditionally tried to control the indigenous relationship with the dead, extirpating what they see as idolatries and defining the proper manner for communicating with the dead (Abercrombie 1998; Silverblatt 1987). Against this background, I think, the Salasacas' control over the send-off of the souls is remarkable, and best seen as appropriation of church power.

The other question is whether it makes sense to view the list of souls as a form of resistance. It is tempting to say that the cooling of the souls and imitation of church archives represents a millenarian impulse among the Salasacas to control their own relationships with the dead, one of the major functions of any religion. The Day of the Dead (and

other death rituals) could be seen as James Scott's (1990) rituals of reversal, if not as raucous as Carnival, similar at least in the sense of turning the world upside down in key respects and offering an ideological
basis for possible revolt. Such an interpretation, however, doesn't fit well
in this case. The church largely retains control over the rituals: the feast-
ing in the cemetery is all done under the clergy's watchful eye, Mass is
well attended, and nobody doubts the efficacy of holy water in cooling
off the souls nor is anyone even trying to criticize the church. Salasacas
aren't like the Yekuana, an Amazonian group that associates writing and
priests with death (Guss 1986:424). To the contrary, the Salasacas actively mimic the church, and, as Michael Brown (1991:401) reminds us
in his critique of resistance studies, imitation is the sincerest form of
flattery. What Brown says about Amazonian millenarian movements
would apply equally to the Day of the Dead: "[I]n Amazonian millenarian movements we see robust efforts to wrestle control of Christianity
from whites while reshaping it to meet the spiritual needs of Indian
peoples. . . . Vigorous appropriation of Christianity is consistent with a
view that ritual knowledge is something to be exchanged and shared"
(ibid.). The list of souls is best viewed as such an effort "to wrestle control of Christianity"; while still a power move, this appropriation does
not entail the same degree of critique and revolutionary potential implied by the term "resistance."

MAGICAL WRITING
IN COMPARATIVE PERSPECTIVE

Archival writing appears in diverse Salasaca beliefs, always with life-and-
death powers, whether to kill and save people (San Gonzalo's book), determine dates of death (God's book), or cool and remember the dead
(the list of souls). Salasaca beliefs thus support Joanne Rappaport's argument about literacy's importance in indigenous Latin American cultures:
"For the past 450 years Indians have participated in the literate conventions of the dominant society, employed the written word as a bridge between community and state, and looked to the archive as a window onto
the struggles of their forebears" (Rappaport 1994a:97–98).[13] In addition,

Salasaca beliefs are rooted in experiences with church writing, especially baptism books that construct personal and Christian identities.

What emerges is a picture of writing as a fundamental symbol of power, so fundamental that it can stand beside more well-studied symbolic forms as a window into indigenous relations with outside society. As an extended example, let me compare the Salasacas' literacy beliefs with Andean origin myths. Roger Rasnake's discussion of the Yura (1988b), a Quechua-speaking group from highland Bolivia, serves as a good example, since the myths he examines are typical of those prevalent throughout the Andes (see Turner 1988:258; Whitten 1988:296). The first such Yura myth is set in a pre-social world, where people called Chullpas planted rocks for crops, lived by moonlight, and worshipped the moon as their god.[14] The Chullpas were vanquished, though, by Tyusninchis, the Yuras' own god of the sun. Tyusninchis then created the Olden People, who named the nearby mountain peaks and made the fields that the Yura plant today. In a second myth, Tyusninchis, in human form, is chased by Spanish devils. Tyusninchis asks a man what he is doing, and the man rudely answers, "What's it look like I'm doing? I'm planting rocks." Tyusninchis leaves the man, saying, "Ah, so be it," and journeys on until he sees another man, to whom he poses the same question. This man, more respectful than the first, answers, "Oh, my lord, I'm planting all the things we eat, maize, potatoes, uqa, broad beans." "Good," answers Tyusninchis. "Now if some men come by on horses asking about me, you tell them that you saw me when you were planting this field." "Very good, sir, I'll do that," the man replies. The next day that man found that all of his crops grew miraculously high overnight: "The corn is tall and ready to be harvested; the potatoes are ready to be dug." When the Spanish devils rode by and asked this man if he saw a young boy (that is, Tyusninchis) pass through, he said yes, he saw the boy when he was planting his field. The devils concluded, "Oh, no, that must have been months ago. Look, the field is ready to be harvested. Let's turn back; he has escaped us." Tyusninchis' trick worked. The third, final myth is also about Spaniards chasing Tyusninchis, who this time takes the form of the Inca King. The Spaniards succeed in catching and killing the Inca, but not before he manages to hide all of his precious metals inside the mountains; to this day, neither the Spaniards nor the Yura have been able to recover those hidden treasures.

What could these stories about rocks, crops, and low-speed chases have to do with Salasaca literacy? At first glance these might seem like apples and oranges, but they are actually more like Macintoshes and Granny Smiths. Literacy beliefs, just like Andean myths, are centrally concerned with the problem of social domination. Salasacas cannot kill San Gonzalo, but he can kill them; they cannot make God alter his book, but his book decides when they die. These writings are beyond Salasaca control, especially God's book. Salasaca literacy beliefs resemble Andean myths, and not just at a formal level, but in terms of their specific message about powerlessness in the face of social inequality and domination.[15]

Literacy symbolism also has to be treated with the same openness to complexity required in other studies.[16] Rasnake analyzed three separately narrated myths and went on to consider rituals like Corpus Christi, complicating the myth with a greater sense of Tyusninchi's semi-autonomous role. Treating any of the myths in isolation would have been misleading. And just as we wouldn't look at a single myth without considering related myths and rituals, we have to look at instances of writing symbolism in tandem. It would be a mistake to look only at God's book, for example, and conclude that the Salasacas flatly accept literacy and, by extension, church and state power. While this interpretation makes sense in this one case, the list of souls provides a different impression. Here, the Salasacas take control of writing, not just in having the lists sprinkled with holy water to cool the dead souls, but also in saving the lists to imitate church archives, appropriating church power for an indigenous send-off of the dead souls. And the list of souls differs fundamentally from San Gonzalo's book in that the former is used for good (remembering the dead souls), while the latter is used for evil (killing people through witchcraft), opposite poles of the moral spectrum.

No single response can be treated as the entire Salasaca perspective, and the full range of responses cannot be comfortably fit into a resistance paradigm. A more appropriate approach is to look at literacy in terms of the anthropology of power: the study of native conceptions of power relations, the way subordinate peoples understand and represent to themselves their experiences with powerful others, through myth, folklore, ritual, devil pacts, humor, and other symbolic forms.[17] Such an approach allows greater flexibility in locating the connections between literacy and power.

Salasaca responses are not even exhausted by the three name lists. In fact, one of the major responses to writing takes place every day in Salasaca classrooms, where students are learning to read and write. The next chapter discusses, among other things, acquisition of these literacy skills with the help of a mountain spirit.

Notes

1. Unfortunately, I did not get to speak with any of the families chasing the lists that day, only others who commented on the scene and the uses of the lists in general.

2. The Day of the Dead, coming at a time of abundance of food in the Andean agricultural cycle, contrasts with fiestas from December to March that can be traced to a lack of certainty about food supplies, as Belote and Belote (1977b) have shown in the case of the Saraguros.

3. As Mary Weismantel points out, there are actually significant differences between the Mexican and Ecuadorian rituals: "In contrast, the same date in Mexico finds no bread babies, no black gruels; the streets are filled instead with vendors of sugar skulls and toy skeletons, colorful and macabre" (1991:868). I return below to the bread babies and gruels, as well as Weismantel's analysis of them.

   My discussion here does not apply to the Evangelical minority (roughly less than 1 percent of the Salasaca population), who do not attend the Catholic Mass, use name lists, or consume alcohol in the cemetery. I also refer here to the cathedral in Pelileo, though a few years ago the parish priest started holding the Mass in the Salasaca church itself. From what I heard and saw, only a handful of people attended this service, while the overwhelming majority went to the Pelileo church. Since the colonial period, the Pelileo church has been the center of Salasaca ritual observance, a tradition continued during the Day of the Dead. The Pelileo church is also preferable because it is located next to the old cemetery. Furthermore, traveling to Pelileo is consistent with spatial orientation to the other world, as indicated in the chapter on God's book.

4. The priest later said he'd heard the same thing.

5. Salasacas have added written lists to these more traditional methods for cooling souls.

6. Such use of intermediaries to gain access to literacy is common in Latin America, not to mention other parts of the world. See, for example, Kalman's (1999) study of scribes in Mexico City and Condori Chura and Ticona Alejo's history (1992) of indigenous Bolivian scribes.

7. There were only two exceptions. One woman wanted her list recopied because of its improper red color, an exception that proved the rule about the importance of black ink. Another woman asked to recopy a tattered old list with about twenty names, some of which she couldn't remember. Her recopied list was the closest thing to literate mnemonics I witnessed that day. Although I never met anyone else who said they had a list that long, a few old people were reported to have had long lists that got recopied. Nobody was sure why, but they speculated it was because these people were very forgetful. In this and other regards, the lists are not standardized. Although such lack of standardization may defy Western expectations about written lists, it is not surprising given the lists' basis in decentralized, family practices; from this perspective, it is remarkable how much standardization does exist. The recopied lists are not included in the immediately following discussion, but they fit entirely within the subsequent analysis of lists as imitators of church archives.

8. There is a tendency to put male names before female, but not always. About half the wives put their relatives' names on separate lists; the other half put their names together with their husband's, usually in separate sections of the list, but in a few cases husbands' and wives' relatives were mixed together and ordered chronologically according to date of death. One of the consistent rules for all lists, in fact, is that the names move down the page from oldest to most recently deceased family members, with the exception of the young children *(angelitos)*, who can appear earlier in the list. The list does not normally include cousins, uncles, aunts, nephews, or nieces, since the closest, living, elder relatives should include those people on their lists. This elder relative is known as the "trunk" *(tronco)*, the same term used in Cumbal, Colombia for familial descent and written genealogies (Rappaport 1994a:73). The basic five-generational kinship model with ego at the center resembles the Inca kinship model analyzed by Zuidema (1977).

9. This difference is reflected in the terms that describe the lists' oral rendition. God "calls" *(cayan)* your name when it is time for you to die, and the San Gonzalo owner "calls" *(cayan)* victims' names. Significantly, witches also "call" victims' names, saying, for example, "Juan, come here, come here" *(Juan, shami, shami)*. On the other hand, the priest's reading of the list of souls is never described as "calling," but rather as "praying"*(rizina* or *liina)*.

10. Although store receipts fulfill the same authorization function, they are not given with most purchases (i.e., those in the marketplace); land titles, as well as receipts for purchases of large items like televisions, are exceptions. The list also resembles the authentification function of Peruvian letters described by Sarah Skar: "As I have learned to appreciate among Matapuqenians, the letter really serves as an object of trust, authenticating the oral message which the courier delivers. In many cases I would say that the letter is the authenticating symbolic object and helps solve the problem of communication at a distance" (1994:271). Rappaport and Cummins (1994:99–103) describe a similar indigenous focus on writing's symbolic form rather than content in their analysis of a sixteenth-century, Indian burial with a papal bull and eighteenth-century messianic uses of letters. And if "authentication" is more broadly defined as uses of literacy as a symbol of power and privilege, much of Rappaport's corpus (especially Rappaport 1987, 1998 [1990], 1994c, and Rappaport and Cummins 1994), along with the work of Gruzinski 1993 [1988] and others, is relevant here.

11. The bread made in these stores in Ambato is famous in other parts of Ecuador, even inspiring imitation north of Quito (Fuentes Roldán 1969:162).

12. The spatial orientation and temporal organization is also the same in both rituals: movement proceeds from the home, to the church and cemetery (facing Mt. Tungurahua, the direction the dead souls travel), and back to the home, where the final send-off of the souls occurs. On the role of drinking and eating to excess to communicate with other beings, see Allen (1988:151–175).

Another Salasaca ritual with bread babies is the Caporales fiesta (known elsewhere as the fiesta of Three Kings), in which the Caporal's partner carries two bread babies on his back, saves them in his house for a year, then brings them to the Caporal's house, where a funeral mass is said and the bread gets buried, with the Caporal's wife crying for her baby (see Corr 2000:158–166; 2002:15–18). When I attended one of these burials at Alonso's uncle's house, the priest, who was brought to the house to say Mass, berated the attendees for lying on the ground in a drunken stupor. The priest demanded, "How many of you here have a Bible?" At first nobody answered, but then one man shouted "A bottle, yes!" (¡Una botella, sí!) and everyone broke out laughing. Although not typical of the bread babies' burial, this interaction reminded me of the element of parody present in the "Head Mass."

13. This also confirms Tristan Platt's (1992:136) suggestion that "the myth of the archive," far from being limited to creole, literary elites (e.g., readers of García Márquez), "has also struck firm roots in the consciousness of the Andean 'people called indians.'" On indigenous literacy and the state, see, for example, Abercrombie (1998); Condori Chura and Ticona Alejo (1992); Guevara-Gil and Salomon (1994); Gruzinski (1993)[1988]; and Platt (1992).

14. The myth texts summarized here are found in Rasnake (1988b:143–146). Some of the quotations here come from those texts, and are mixed with Rasnake's own glosses on figures in the myths.

15. Salasacas, too, have stories about chthonic mountain powers who withhold gold from the Spaniards, one of the most common of which holds that the Inca Rumiñahui, before he was killed, hid his gold in nearby mountains; nobody since, neither Spanish colonialist, Ecuadorian white, or gringo scientist or adventurer, has ever found the gold, and the mountains have killed many who have tried. Corr (2000) perceptively analyzes many examples of mountain powers, including stories about hidden treasure, and Whitten (1988) provides an excellent discussion of chthonic features common throughout South America.

16. Critiques of Taussig (1980) include Gross (1983); McEachern and Mayer (1986); Platt (1983); Roseberry (1989); Trouillot (1986); and Turner (1986). I have focused here on writing only because it has received less attention in the past, but ideally the multiple symbols of power would be considered in conjunction.

17. For important calls for such research, see Anderson (1990) and Geertz (1980). Carried out under various theoretical headings in Latin America,

this research includes studies of ethnic humor (Bricker 1973), "fat cutters" (Canessa 2000; Weismantel 2001), mountain powers (Lyons 1999; Rasnake 1988a–b), and myths, histories, and rituals that focus on power and ethnicity (Gelles et al. 1996; Gose 1994; Hill [ed.] 1988; Rivera Cusicanqui 1986; Rogers [ed.] 1998; Salomon 1981; Urban and Sherzer [eds.] 1991; Wachtel 1977; Warren 1989 [1978]; Weismantel 2001). Studies of millenarianism are also relevant here, and see Sutton (1994) on the way studies of positional identities assume binary views of self and other.

6

Weaving and Writing

Europeans and North Americans often assume that writing preserves information better than "oral memory"—hence the reliance on archives, as the true record of events—but this taken-for-granted view can be turned on its head by other cultural perspectives. Consider, for example, one Native North American student's response to her teacher, who was about to stress writing's superior mnemonic capacities:

> I [the teacher] once said in a class that a significant difference between the spoken word and the written word was one of permanence. A student, an Inupiaq-English bilingual woman, said that comment had explained something she had tried to explain to us for a long time. As she put it, "When you say something, that's permanent; it doesn't go away. But when you write it, it's just on a piece of paper which anyone can tear up and throw away." [Scollon 1994:215]

For this student, writing is ephemeral, speaking is permanent. In Salasaca, I have observed a similar reversal of European/North American assumptions. It is not that the Salasacas explicitly celebrate the virtues of oral memory or deny writing's ability to preserve certain forms of information. Nonetheless, when Europeans and North Americans most expect to find faith in written mnemonics—when comparing weaving and writing—the Salasacas frustrate these expectations. This became clear to me when I observed the chasm between views of indigenous weavings held by tourists and the Salasacas themselves.

I have had ample opportunities to observe these differences while staying with Alonso, since tourists regularly visit his house to learn about his weavings. Most of these visitors are from the United States and Western Europe; they are often young people taking long backpack trips throughout South America, married couples on short vacations, or students and development workers who are traveling with friends and relatives; everyone is college-educated and middle or upper-middle class. Alonso lives right off the main road to Baños, a popular stopping point on the way to the Amazon, so it's easy for people to stop nearby and walk up the path to his house (see Figure 1.1). During these visits, Alonso discusses his weaving, all of which is created on a backstrap loom with designs that derive from the large *chumbi* belt. By any standards, this belt is one of the most traditional aspects of Salasaca dress: its designs and backstrap-loom weaving techniques were brought to the indigenous inhabitants of Ecuador by the conquering Incas, in the fifteenth century (Meisch and Rowe 1998:44–47); it is still worn daily by Salasaca women, to hold up their heavy black skirts; and it is worn by both men and women on important ceremonial occasions like the Day of the Dead (see Figure 6.1 and Figure 1.8).[1]

During the discussions I was present for, I heard the same questions asked over and over: "What do these mean?"—asked while pointing to *chumbi* designs like the one in Figure 6.2—"What story do they tell?" Some version of these questions was asked by virtually everyone, wherever they were from and whatever their background. The underlying idea was that both weaving and writing are material repositories for important information and narratives—a type of archive in cloth.[2] Though nobody thought the weavings encoded specific spoken words the way alphabetic writing does, the tourists often explicitly referred to Alonso's weaving as a type of writing or the counterpart to European/North American (alphabetic) writing. This is a perfectly logical comparison for Europeans and North Americans, but not Salasacas, who throw off European/North American expectations by saying that writing and weaving are similar only because they're both hard to learn. The equation between writing

Figure 6.1   Alonso working on the backstrap loom, with chumbi *belts and other weavings behind him. Photo by Dennis Pippen.*

and weaving, so intuitively comprehensible, actually tells us more about European/North American than Salasaca culture.

SALASACA COMPARISONS
BETWEEN WEAVING AND WRITING

Although comparisons between weaving and writing were never a big topic of conversation among Salasacas, and some people had clearly never even thought about it, others agreed there was a similarity when asked. But contrary to European/North American expectations, they did *not* mention mnemonic qualities; their response was essentially, "Yes, they're both hard" *(ishquindij jinchi gan).* A couple of elderly women used this exact phrase, and many middle-aged people said something similar or had heard such comparisons made by their grandparents. As one elderly man put it, "They're both hard to do. There's a lot to remember, and you

Figure 6.2   A chumbi belt design of an Inca dancer. Photo by Dennis Pippen.

have to go slowly." The focus, in other words, is on the process, not the product, of weaving and writing. I won't try to recapitulate a detailed weaving lesson, but the following description, from a textile expert's book, gives some sense of what it involves:

> The [weaving] pattern can be achieved in several ways. For example, a blue yarn and a white yarn can be warped alternately, producing horizontal bars. Or, blue yarns can be warped for a while, then white, giving vertical stripes. More complex textiles can be woven using both the warp order and color, and a pick-up technique (*agllana* in Quichua). The weaver uses his fingers or a little wooden stick to pick-up and hold out certain warp threads, to form a design. . . . Weaving on the backstrap loom is slow, since the heddle stick and shed rod must be lifted by hand. If a pick-up design is done, then the process is even slower. And because the warps are set so close together they sometimes stick together causing mistakes. [Meisch 1987:73–74]

Suffice it to say that weaving, with its minute movements and thread counts, is detailed, demanding work, not only for novices but also for experts, who still must exercise concentration and patience in its execution (see Figure 6.3). Weaving's difficulty and exactitude make it a logical point of comparison with writing, especially for people who have only started gaining literacy skills in large numbers in recent decades.

The Salasacas' focus on weaving and writing as skills appeared not just in their responses to my direct questions but also in ritual supplications for both skills. The Salasacas pray to the same mountain site for improvements in writing, weaving, and other tasks demanding fine hand coordination, again revealing an equation between writing and weaving as similar skills, physically and mentally.

The site where these prayers occurs, Nitón Cruz, derives strength not just from its location on a mountain, a typical source of power in the Andes, but also its liminal, betwixt-and-between status.[3] Nitón Cruz is located on the border between Salasaca and the neighboring white town of Pelileo; from the summit, you can actually see Salasaca below and,

Figure 6.3   Close-up of threads and weaving instruments. Photo by Dennis Pippen.

facing the other direction, Pelileo (see Figure 6.4). This is an ethnic threshold, part of the boundary referred to as "our border" or "the indigenous people's border" *(runa lindi)*. It is also literally an "intersection" *(cruz)* between two walking paths, the one that goes north into Pelileo and the one running roughly east-west along a mountain ridge into Nitón, another predominantly white neighboring town. And at the intersection of these paths is Nitón Cruz itself, a small hole, four feet deep and three feet wide, that bears the shape of a cross, with many tiny crosses carved into its dirt walls. Nitón Cruz is a crossroads, then, in more ways than one.

And this crossroads is where Salasacas go if they are having trouble mastering a skill—specifically, spinning, weaving, playing a musical instrument, or writing. Even if someone understands the basic elements of one of these skills, he or she may go to Nitón Cruz to pray to God and the mountain (which amounts to the same thing) for assistance in gaining greater dexterity. Here's the way one woman put it, referring to spinning:

> Up there, at Nitón Cruz, that's where you go if you can't spin wool. The woman goes there with her distaff and spindle. She prepares that, and she spins a little bit of wool, and she leaves that at Nitón Cruz, and then she asks God to help her learn how to weave, how to be a good weaver. She leaves it in that hole, that one up there. And that will help her.

One man said:

> You go there to pray for the ability to weave. You go with a candle, and wash your hands with the wax that comes off it, and leave that candle there. Some people go there with pot shards and wipe their hands with them, and that helps them to weave.

The pot shards this man refers to are left as a form of payment. As the woman notes, a small representative object is also left, such as a tuft of wool for spinning. The various times I checked the site, I also saw tufts of wool on small sticks (for spinning), yarn (for weaving tapestries), and Bic pens and pieces of paper, some blank and others that had been children's homework (for writing and school work).[4]

Figure 6.4   Hilltop near Nitón Cruz, where Salasacas pray for weaving skills.

The same site is used, then, to master skills that require finely coordinated, repetitive hand movements. This explains why the mountain is never called on to help someone cook better, though I sometimes raised this possibility, such as the time a woman was saying Nitón could help people "weave shawls, tapestries, all weavings, and spinning," and I asked, "What about cooking?" The woman said, "No, not cooking; that's just something you learn from your mother; you just do it, even if you can't do it that well." Most importantly, writing and weaving are the two crafts most commonly treated by Nitón, demonstrating their comparability in Salasaca eyes as challenging skills, physically and mentally, requiring the memory of precise hand movements, the sort of unconscious body memory and "practical knowledge" that comes with skill mastery.[5]

But it's not that the Salasacas choose to focus on a process-based equivalence between weaving and writing while ignoring weaving's mnemonic function; the fact is no such function exists in Salasaca, at least not in the sense envisioned by tourists. I never found a single instance in which weaving was used to recall a specific narrative or contribute to an oral performance. Although Salasacas occasionally tell short narratives, especially trickster tales that serve entertainment and etiological purposes, these narratives aren't connected to the traditional belts or any other weavings.[6] The deer design, for example, appears more often than any other in Salasaca *chumbi* belts (Hoffmeyer 1985:345), and deer stories are told in other parts of highland Ecuador (Jara [ed.] 1987 [1982]), yet when I asked Alonso the meaning of his deer design, he did not connect it with an extended narrative. Instead, he provided isolated (albeit fascinating) details about the deer's healing uses. It's not that Alonso's memory failed him (in fact, he remembers stories better than most), it's just that these figures are not linked to extended narratives.[7] Whether or not this was the case in the past, the *chumbi* belts are prized nowadays simply for their aesthetic qualities and depictions of fiesta figures, animals, and other important aspects of rituals and everyday life.[8] Designs are also preserved through the force of tradition, since weavers learn from relatives and reproduce their mentors' designs. Alonso, for example, learned almost all his designs from his father, who in turn learned from his uncle, and Alonso has since passed on his weaving designs to his brothers-in-law, who spent several years weaving by his side (when I refer to Alonso's weaving, I include, in fact, the work of these other weavers). I found essentially the same designs in other expert weavers' repertoires, and the Salasacas themselves said that the *chumbi* designs come from their ancestors and have not changed since the far-distant past (*ñauba timpu munda*).[9] The weaving designs endure, in other words, for their traditional aesthetic, rather than mnemonic, value. In this regard, the Salasacas conform to a wider regional pattern of deemphasized verbal memory in favor of more concretely embodied memory practices (Abercrombie 1998; Rappaport 1994a, 1998 [1990]; Sánchez Parga 1989). As Sánchez Parga (1989:119) explains, this pattern reflects an egalitarian ethos and rejection of ritual languages controlled by a small group of specialists.

Ironically, then, in cases like the witch's book and list of souls, the Salasacas focus on literate mnemonics in ways that most Europeans and North Americans wouldn't predict, yet when it comes to weaving, which Europeans and North Americans most expect to be compared with writing as a mnemonic, such comparisons are not made. The tourists' assumptions about weaving tell us about writing's place in European and

North American—not Salasaca—culture. The Salasacas' weaving-writing comparisons are equally revealing. It's not surprising in itself that native analogs are sought for writing; the same comprehension-by-analogy-with-more-familiar-terms occurs when tourists compare weaving to writing, just as it does when non-Westerners equate alphabetic literacy with indigenous analogs, such as hunting tracks (Perrin 1985), hallucinogenic visions (Gow 1990), visual arts (Brotherston 1981), and weaving (Allen 1997:74; Arnold 1997; March 1983; Rappaport and Cummins 1994; Tedlock and Tedlock 1985). But what makes each analog interesting is the way it highlights certain aspects of writing and obscures others, revealing salient features in native conceptions. Colonial Andean equations between writing and *quipu* knots, for example, treated writing as an object in itself, regardless of its specific contents (Rappaport and Cummins 1994:100).[10] And other cultures have highlighted other aspects, such as Amazonian comparisons with shamanism that configure writing as a special language understood only by a few (Gow 1990).

The Salasaca analogies shed light, in particular, on questions of skill transmission and power appropriation, revealing that the Salasacas don't see writing (or reading or school work in general) as the exclusive domain of whites or an unfamiliar, unattainable skill. Instead, the Salasacas see writing as something comparable to their own weaving skills, something that can be mastered with hard work and, if necessary, the assistance of God and a mountain spirit. A glance at classroom instruction methods shows why this equation is so easily made. Oral transcription and copying of texts are primary methods of instruction not just in Salasaca but in Ecuador's Hispanic education system in general, and not only in primary schools but high schools as well. Gustavo Larrea Cabrera, an Ecuadorian educational sociologist, describes this method of "memorization education" *(educación memorista)* as follows:

> The professors dictate their classes and the students take notes in their notebooks; later, at home, they have to recopy what they wrote in class, the notes and dictations they took, on the basis of which they do the homework assigned by the teacher, for which they will also have the assistance of a written text. At the next class session, the student repeats the lesson orally for the professor and other students. [Larrea Cabrera 1990:110–111]

I observed similar methods of instruction in Salasaca schools. For example, eighth-grade Spanish teachers read out long model sentences, which students then copied into their notebooks in exercises intended to teach new vocabulary. In high school geography and civics classes, too, the teachers dictated—and students transcribed, verbatim—questions and answers, as well as extended definitions of terms like "geography," "universe," "mineral resources," and "Andean Council." In some cases notebooks were handed in for evaluation, but students' notes were generally more important as study material for written and oral exams, in which terms had to be defined as they had been in class. Dictation was even more important in primary school, where students regularly took classes like "Dictation and Writing" *(Clase de Dictado y Redacción)*, getting drilled on penmanship *(las copias, buena letra)*, spelling *(ortografía)*, and dictation skills *(dictado, redacción)*. Because teachers didn't require that students purchase textbooks, citing their prohibitively high costs (upwards of $5), most students didn't own them (in middle school classes of roughly thirty-five students, I never counted more than five students with their own copies of the textbook). However, disposable pens and cheap notebooks, where dictations were recorded and studied, were ubiquitous. Some teachers pointed to the emphasis on dictation as a practical necessity, forced on them by the lack of textbooks, but this method of instruction also has deep roots in church catechism and Ecuador's public education system, with their privileging of word-for-word memorization of written texts (Sánchez Parga 1989:125).[11]

Educators, influenced by Paolo Freire and bilingual education programs, criticize such methods of instruction for their discordance with home-based (usually indigenous) learning: "These methods inevitably conflict with the customs, the culture, with the ideas and values the children have learned at home and in the community" (Larrea Cabrera 1990:50). The Salasaca case, however, shows that such conflict is not inevitable, at least in terms of conceptions of skill transmission. Learning to weave and write is seen as a matter of memorization, repetition, apprenticeship, and fine coordination.

This view of literacy as a familiar, attainable skill underpins increasing Salasaca school enrollments and literacy rates. As noted earlier, Salasaca school attendance has shot up dramatically in recent decades:

47 percent of Salasacas had no schooling in 1974 and 12 percent had only one to three years, whereas by 1994 every Salasaca child completed at least a few years of schooling (every young person over six I met in 1994 had completed or was completing at least three years of schooling). For the most part, these changes are due to the Salasacas' increased involvement in a market economy, including the weaving business, which often requires basic literacy and numerical skills for written communication, receipts, and bookkeeping. Salasaca views of writing as a practical skill, though, also have to be considered part of these changes, for without them the Salasacas might not have embraced education as much as they have. Salasaca attitudes have changed significantly since the 1950s and 1960s, when most parents resisted sending their children to school, only succumbing under the pressure of bribes and police threats. And such educational changes can be considered another appropriation of writing. The Salasacas don't just appropriate writing through magical means like witches' books and lists of souls, they also master writing skills themselves (albeit with an occasional magical boost); they don't just save the lists of souls, they also send their children to school, and these children go on to write the family's list, replacing white scribes. Although literacy skills in themselves do not obliterate more fundamental power inequities, they obviously give Salasacas a higher degree of control over writing.

EUROPEANS/
NORTH AMERICANS AND WRITING

So, where is the tourists' conception of weaving as a mnemonic coming from, if not from the Salasacas themselves? It is clearly not secured from historical accounts of the Incas. Although *chumbi* belts and shirts were an integral part of the Incas' gift economy (Murra 1962) and their elaborate iconography may have referred to sacred narratives about gods and ancestors, nobody has yet been able to decipher the significance of this iconography, and certainly no tourist ever cited attempts to do so. The only historical references I heard were to other indigenous peoples; a few tourists said they knew Native North Americans used wampum belts to remember their stories, so they assumed the same thing happened in Salasaca.

But the primary evidence cited was the form of the weavings themselves. "Just look at it," said a student from Los Angeles, holding one of Alonso's *chumbi* belts. "I mean, you can tell that these pictures must mean *something*. Like this one, it's obviously some kind of animal, probably a dog [said while pointing to a design that Alonso agreed was a dog]. Why else would they have them here?" According to this reasoning, typical of most tourists, the designs obviously represent specific objects or beings (even though it's not always clear exactly what they are, given their distinctive style), so they resemble writing: both stand for something, both convey messages. "It's like we have writing that tells a story and they have weaving that does the same thing," concluded the student. Other tourists pointed out that the designs on the belt appeared one after another, suggesting that they could be read in a linear fashion, from top to bottom, just as we read from left to right. These similarities in form only become noticeable, though, once the premise is accepted that the messages conveyed by the designs are narratives that conserve important information—in other words, that the weavings are like alphabetic writing.

Far from outlandish or even surprising, this reasoning makes perfect sense—and that's the point. People try to comprehend novelties through comparisons with their own culture, and, for Europeans and North Americans, the most obvious counterpart to realistic, pictorial weaving is alphabetic writing. This is a logical conclusion, coming as they/we do from a culture that is so reliant on literacy as a mnemonic. The U.S. court system, in fact, privileges written over oral memory (e.g., Clifford 1988), as does the education system, most notably in the discipline of history (Thompson 1988[1978]:23). I include myself and other anthropologists here, since we would all be lost without our fieldnotes. As Jean Jackson found, anthropologists variously regard their fieldnotes as everything from rites of passage to garbage—yet none doubts the notes' mnemonic value: "While fieldnotes' superior recall is acknowledged as an aid, they are nonetheless resented and sometimes envied for being more accurate [than oral memory]" (Jackson 1995:49). You don't have to be an academic, though, to equate writing and memory; it's simply part of the European/North American cultural bias in favor of literacy (Keller Cohen 1993). Whether using palm pilots or shopping lists, Europeans and North Americans instinctively trust writing's superior recall ability.

Since the colonial period, in fact, Europeans and North Americans have compared native weaving and other mnemonic systems to alphabetic writing.[12] Early colonial Spanish writers had an easier time assimilating Mexican paintings, for example, with their notions of "books" than they did comprehending the non-textual, tactile aspect of *quipus,* the Incan system of recording information through knotted weavings (Mignolo 1995:86). Tourists at Alonso's house are similarly drawn to the realistic iconography in his weavings, but few ask about the possible meaning of abstract, non-pictorial patterns (e.g., Arnold 1997; Cereceda 1986; Cummins 1994; Rappaport and Cummins 1994), or about non-textual memory practices, such as libation sequences, land possession ceremonies, and staff rituals (Abercrombie 1998; Rappaport 1994a). The point is not to take the tourists to task for not knowing about these non-textual memory practices, which have only recently been exposed by research specialists.[13] Rather, the point is simply that European/North American assumptions about writing and memory have a long, deep-seated history.

Yet perhaps the references to colonialism are not far afield. Certainly a book like this raises troubling questions about the power of cultural representations, about speaking for another culture and consuming and reproducing images of it. Especially in a book about literacy and power, I would be remiss if I simply looked at Ecuadorian bureaucratic writing and ignored the power dynamics underlying my own writing, if I didn't recognize that my own writing may have as much power as any other the Salasacas have encountered thus far. Just as a baptism book can define existence, so, too, can a book like this one if it promotes stereotypes among tourists and European/North American readers.

Various studies, Edward Said's *Orientalism* (1978) being the best-known, have shown that anthropology and other sciences have produced essentialist, binary oppositions, us-them contrasts that imprison cultural others in their European/North American terms. Middle Easterners are imagined as corrupt despots, exotic women, and honor-obsessed males,

North and South American Indians as noble warriors, spiritual sages, and bloodthirsty cannibals. As David Murray puts it, "What is lost thereby is diversity. The thousand native worlds . . . become a two-step sideshow. . . . [B]e they fallen or ennobled, we have defined the Indian by our essential opposition" (Murray 1991:83). This critique is taken so seriously (as it should be) that anthropologists and anyone else who represents other cultures are now regarded with suspicion. Anthropology classes watch films like *Cannibal Tours* (O'Rourke 1987), a documentary about tourists traveling up the Sepik River in Papua New Guinea, still in pursuit of cannibal images and confirmation for their stereotypes.[14] The film doesn't cite Said or explicitly condemn the tourists in a voice-over, but it doesn't have to; with their essentialist notions, insensitive gawking, and obvious affluence, the tourists are clearly the bad guys. Dean MacCannell (1992:20), a prominent critic of tourism, also makes it clear who the bad guys are when he refers to tourists like these as "*metaphoric cannibals*," using "cannibal" in a non-sympathetic sense.

Any representations of indigenous attitudes toward alphabetic writing, in particular, run the risk of reproducing stereotypes of primitive others, given writing's role as a symbol of Western civilization and science and orality's antithetical association with paganism and magical thought: "only early modern European civilisation came to make its own ability properly to describe and understand the other, its own proper literacy, into the very definition of its own identity as against the rest of the world" (Harbsmeier 1985:72). Anthropology itself was largely founded on oral-literate contrasts (Certeau 1988), which is why when people hear I'm an anthropologist, they sometimes ask if I study "tribes" or "non-literate people," the presumed safer term for isolated, non-European/North American peoples. I am aware, then, that representing Salasaca views of writing carries serious risks.

It's hard to know for certain whether my book will perpetuate stereotypes, but my experience several years ago with a pamphlet about Alonso's weavings may serve as a partial predictor. Even if it doesn't, that pamphlet's production provides an interesting case study in itself of the power dynamics entailed in European/North American writing, mnemonics, and cultural representation. To interpret those dynamics, I have to back up to the time before Alonso and I met, before Alonso even decided to become a weaver.

A Tourist Pamphlet

As of the late 1980s, Alonso didn't weave *chumbis,* but his father, José Pilla Curichumbi, did. Unfortunately, José did not make a good living weaving for other Salasacas, even by local standards, and he had to supplement his work with farming. Having few other options, in the early 1990s Alonso therefore did what many Salasacas have done before and since: he took up construction work on the Galápagos Islands, building houses for wage labor. Alonso would probably be working in construction to this day if he had not realized that he could possibly support himself by selling *chumbis* to outsiders. This possibility first started to dawn on Alonso after several North Americans admired and purchased his father's *chumbis,* including a Peace Corps volunteer and two U.S. anthropologists, Lynn Meisch (1987) and Laura Miller (1998). Within the same time period, Alonso met an owner of a folk arts store in Quito who agreed to buy several of his father's belts. The owner realized that most tourists wouldn't buy his father's traditional belt, since it was too wide to function as a belt for Western-style pants and too small for a wall hanging, so she advised Alonso to convert the *chumbi* into bracelets. Stimulated by this and other advice, Alonso gave up construction work, came back to Salasaca, and with his father started to make bracelets and items like key chains and thin belts.

Although his father died shortly afterward, Alonso continued weaving on his own, struggling to make a living with the skills his father had handed down. When I first met Alonso in 1994 (through an introduction by the departing Peace Corps volunteer), he was always happy to talk with me, pulling out his best (in fact, his only) chair for me to sit on and inviting me to share meals with him and his family. Sometimes he kept weaving during our conversations, as he would later when I moved in with him, but most of the time he would stop and come sit next to me, his speech polite but direct as we roamed up one conversation path, back out, and down another.

I stepped willy-nilly into the former Peace Corps volunteer's role, offering advice about designs and gringo aesthetics, but the biggest chal-
lenge was to find a way to sell all these products. Seeing the bags of
weavings pile up inside his house, I realized Alonso was doing better at
producing than promoting his merchandise. He occasionally sold weavings to the store in Quito and to visiting friends of the new Peace Corps
volunteer, but otherwise he had no regular sales outlet. Then one afternoon I came up with an idea: He had weaving and I had writing, and we
both liked to analyze Salasaca culture, so why not make a small pamphlet about his weavings? Although it wasn't clear this plan would work,
Alonso agreed it was worth trying, so for the next several weeks I tape-
recorded interviews with him, asking him to tell me everything he could
think of about each design in his repertoire. Alonso took this project seriously and participated enthusiastically. With only the slightest prods
from me, he filled up hours of tape and opened my eyes to intriguing aspects of the culture, from the rattle made from goat-fingernails to the
cure for spirit attacks made from a deer's horn. In my own house at
night (I hadn't moved in with Alonso yet), my wife sketched out each
design in pencil, and I typed up summaries of what Alonso had told me
about the corresponding designs. When Alonso and I agreed everything
was ready, I printed out a final copy on my dot-matrix printer, glued in
the pencil sketches, and went to the city to have twenty copies made and
stapled together. This was a cheap, low-tech operation, but as such, it
could easily be repeated by Alonso in the future, since I gave him the
originals (see Figure 6.5).

Meanwhile, we had posted a sign in the courtyard, painting "Señor
Alonso Pilla" with red letters and a white background on an old piece of
wood; and Alonso had been busy generating contacts with the managers
of tourist restaurants and hotels, who agreed to direct tourists to his
house. Within a few weeks, Alonso started receiving foreign visitors, and
since that time he has sold most of his weavings to such visitors.
Although these sales are not overwhelmingly large, they have allowed
Alonso to support himself and his extended family.[15]

Alonso was half-surprised and glad to tell me that the first visitor had
bought the pamphlet, and since almost every subsequent visitor has
done the same, he has come to see the pamphlet as an integral part of

Figure 6.5   Alonso examining the illustrations from the first draft of the pamphlet. Photo by Dennis Pippen.

his business. Yet Alonso's "success" has been primarily due to the quality of his weaving, his charm and openness, and his analytical proclivities. Alonso has essentially become an anthropologist, an interpreter of his culture, and the pamphlet, no work of art, is only one small part of a larger picture.

The pamphlet interests me in this context, though, for what it reveals about the possible effects of my writing about Salasaca. For example, the pamphlet has lent anthropological validation to Alonso's weaving, not only by converting Alonso's words into something tangible, but by demonstrating that I find these weavings interesting enough to write about. Alonso has noticed the tone of recognition and interest that often shows through in tourists' voices when he mentions the word "anthropologist" *(antropólogo)* and describes how I wrote this pamphlet.[16] The tourists assume that an anthropologist wouldn't study this weaving unless it had some cultural noteworthiness; and I do believe that and say as much in the pamphlet. Also, for those few tourists who do not speak Spanish, the pamphlet may be their only route to understanding Alonso's weaving. And the pamphlet provides all tourists with a way to remember the meaning of each design.

These effects notwithstanding, the pamphlet has not undermined Alonso's authority, from what I've seen. This story is not like the one about the anthropologist who asks the native to tell him all about his traditional culture, at which point the native says, "No problem," goes to the back room, and brings out a copy of a classic ethnography written forty years earlier about his tribe. Alonso does bring out the pamphlet for inquiring visitors, but that doesn't inhibit him from interpreting his culture any way he cares to. He doesn't have any reason to defer to the pamphlet, which, after all, only contains his own words in paraphrased English. The pamphlet has not ossified his interpretations, contrary to the sort of writing-is-death notion that James Clifford (1986) finds rooted in European/North American culture. David Sutton shows, for example, that people from Western cultures often resist transferring their cooking knowledge into written form; as one Greek-American woman remarked, "a week after the recipes were written down, my grandmother was dead."[17] Without fearing obsolescence now that his words are written down, Alonso continues to reformulate his interpretations regardless of what the pamphlet says. In fact, he doesn't even re-read the pamphlet (since he doesn't speak English), nor have I rehearsed its contents since I first translated it back to him, so it makes no special claim on his opinions: if anything, it bolsters rather than reduces his authority.

STEREOTYPES

The trickier question is whether the pamphlet perpetuates stereotypes of primitive others. The tourists often assume the stories told by the weavings are myths, so it's possible that I am helping reproduce long-standing dichotomies between the West, the place of true, rational, history, and the non-West, the place of supernatural myths. My pamphlet may leave this impression by attaching meaning to the designs, implying that they do tell a mythic story after all. Moreover, my very existence as an anthropologist, enacted and registered in the pamphlet, may perpetuate all the usual distinctions between writing and orality, reason and magic, the West and the Rest.

I recognize these dangers, but believe they are minimized for two reasons. First, the tourists never acted surprised or disappointed when Alonso wrote down their addresses. They did not believe that because he had his own pen and paper, he had no place in an oral Garden of Eden.

More important, Alonso himself never expressed any feeling that he was being looked at in a demeaning manner; quite the opposite, he has thrived on the tourists' and my intense interest in his culture. The overwhelming effect of this attention has been to stimulate Alonso's pride in his culture and consciousness of it as such. In the first few months of our friendship, Alonso used to say to me, delighted and half amazed, "It's a rebirth of the culture!" And of course if you consider his biography, you can understand why he feels this way: he went from working construction to rescuing the art of his father, who had been one of the best *chumbi* weavers in the village and whose talents and designs would have been lost if Alonso hadn't maintained them.[18] To become an expert weaver, it's not enough to simply gain rudimentary skills in a few sessions; those skills have to be honed and perfected through repeated practice. Because of these time demands, most Salasacas, as well as other Ecuadorian Indians like the Otavaleños (Meisch 1987:140), lament that *chumbi*-weaving skills are being lost in the younger generations. Alonso, by contrast, has been given an opportunity to perfect his skills, first by apprenticing with his father and then through his daily weaving for tourists. Inspired by their enthusiasm, Alonso has even recently built a hostel on his mother's farm, so that the discussions can last even longer, and he and his extended family can demonstrate other aspects of their culture, including Andean cuisine, folk music (Alonso is now passionately involved as a flute player for a local band that performs for tourist visits and Salasaca weddings), and tours of local mountain sites.[19] Far from a demeaning, last alternative, Alonso's work with the tourists has been deeply fulfilling (at least thus far), allowing him to reach back into his past while maturing into an expert weaver, teacher, and musician.

And this is not a unique situation. Terence Turner, for example, describes similar effects among indigenous Brazilian groups studied by anthropologists: "As a general point, for many native peoples, the fact that anthropologists and other relatively prestigious outsiders, who plainly disposed of impressive resources by local Brazilian as well as native standards, were prepared to spend their resources, not to mention much of their lives, on the study of native 'cultures,' may have done more than anything else to convey to these people the awareness that their traditional way of life and ideas were phenomena of great value and interest in the eyes of at least some sectors of the alien enveloping society" (Turner 1991:301).[20]

Yet critiques of tourism and stereotypes often fail to consider such perspectives, the opinions of the very people ostensibly being defended. Alonso's case therefore raises a more general point: whether the people in question reject or welcome outsiders' images has to count for something in any critical evaluation. At the very least, it is important to recognize that well-intentioned academic positions can be profoundly at odds with those of native peoples. Mary Weismantel (1991) makes a similar point when she notes that, just at the moment when indigenous revitalization movements have started to celebrate a pan-Indian, Inca heritage, academics have rejected the idea of a shared Andean culture as an essentialist fiction. Similarly, Christopher Tilley (1997) finds the "critical sociology of tourism" literatures contradicted by Melanesians' own desires to represent and preserve their cultures through touristic performances. As Tilley puts it, rather than asking whether a tourist performance is an authentic tradition, "It would seem to be more fruitful to ask: what kind of image are these people self-consciously constructing of themselves? and whom do they wish to be?" (Tilley 1997:84). In Alonso's case, a traditional weaver is precisely who he wants to be.

My experience with the pamphlet therefore gives me some basis for guarded optimism about the effects of this book. Nonetheless, I know the two writings differ in important ways. Compared to the pamphlet, this book is more my own academic interpretation, one not necessarily tied to a face-to-face encounter in which the Salasacas speak for themselves. And rather than focusing on weaving, a celebrated art form, this book delves into views of magical literacy, so it could easily reinforce European/North American preconceptions of Latin American Indians as simple people caught up in magical beliefs because they don't understand how writing really works. This book enters more treacherous territory than the pamphlet.

Anyone who has read this far, however, should realize I have been arguing that Salasacas astutely comprehend writing. Far from naive peoples unfamiliar with literacy, Salasacas have penetrated archival literacy's essence in Ecuador, perceiving its use as a mnemonic device based on lists of names and dates and its connection to church and state power. Even without mastering the technical aspects of literacy until recently, they have discerned its uses, ideologies, and social relations as well or better than most literate Europeans and North Americans, in the same way that other disenfranchised peoples familiarize themselves with the power that consistently tramples them.

The entire thrust of this book is to show that writing is an integral part of Salasaca culture, not an extraneous force confined to urban centers and the anthropologist's fieldnotes, nor a modern influence that will automatically corrupt a pristine oral environment. This is not a story about a tribe that has just encountered writing for the first time, such as Claude Lévi-Strauss's famous description of a Brazilian chief imitating writing to impress his tribesmen (1981). While such first-contact accounts seem to reveal primeval truths, baring each culture's essential nature in a single dramatic moment, they are deceptive anomalies: few if any indigenous groups have been removed from writing over the past five centuries. Nonetheless, indigenous views of literacy were airbrushed out of anthropological accounts until recently, perhaps in the interest of maintaining images of pristine cultures, or what one scholar calls the "baptized but not evangelized" view of Andean culture (Abercrombie 1998). As recently as the mid-1990s, Joanne Rappaport could accurately report that "Scholars have virtually ignored indigenous literacy, despite the fact that for the past 450 years Indians have participated in the literate conventions of the dominant society, employed the written word as a bridge between community and state, and looked to the archive as a window onto the struggles of their forebears" (Rappaport 1994a:98). Pursuing the opening created by Rappaport and others, I have made literacy the central focus here, and I believe that doing so, despite the risks involved, provides a realistic picture of Salasaca culture.[21]

Notes

1. Alonso weaves a belt known in Quichua as the *chumbi,* the type of weaving that is the focus of this chapter. There are actually four types of *chumbi* belts: the *senidur, frutilla, mushaiyuj,* and *yanga chumbi.* The *yanga chumbi* (meaning "cheap, ordinary belt" in Quichua) is bought from other indigenous groups, usually the Otavaleños (and thus also known as *Otavalo chumbi*). The *senidur* (literally, "Senator," Sp./Q.) is a simple belt with two parallel lines running down its center, often a red background with two white lines, and was the most popular belt for men in the past (unlike the others, this belt is only worn by men), but nowadays the *senidur chumbi* is rarely seen, even on ceremonial occasions. Another popular belt for both men and women is the *frutilla chumbi,* which owes its name to the series of strawberries (*frutilla,* Sp./Q.)—that is, strawberry-like designs—that run vertically along its center. In this chapter, however, I am specifically concerned with the *mushaiyuj chumbi,* i.e., "belt with representational designs" (Q.), because it is the basis of Alonso's weavings, tourist comments on them, and, unless otherwise noted, the Salasacas' comparisons between weaving and writing discussed below. For a description of *chumbis* and other Salasaca weavings, such as shawls, see Miller (1998:126–143).

2. To make sure the underlying idea was indeed a textual model, I sometimes asked visitors if the weavings reminded them of anything from their/our culture, or dropped the point that Salasacas compare their weaving to writing, waiting for them to finish my thought with their own details. Most people said something about weaving and writing being alike as ways of remembering, especially once I first brought up the weaving-writing comparison. As one thirty-seven-year-old white male from Manhattan (a restaurant owner) said, "Yeah, I can see that [that weaving and writing are compared]. I mean, they're both for remembering things, right? It's like these are their books." Another North American, a middle-aged woman from Boston, said, "Well, the weaving really is a kind of writing, like the way we have books and papers and everything." Meisch and Rowe also note that "Written texts are so important in our own society that it seems natural to make this comparison" (Meisch and Rowe 1998:39); the comparison they refer to involves Western metaphors of weaving as a language of social messages—about social status, gender, age, marital status—that can be read like text.

3. Nitón Cruz specifically derives power from its contiguity with Quinlli Urcu, a mountain that assists healing rituals, gives strength through dreams to fiesta leaders who sleep there, brings water during drought (though nowadays it is characterized as a lazy "sleepy-head" [*puñisiqui*] because it no longer brings sufficient rainfall), and increases and decreases human, animal, and plant fertility, among other things. Some older informants reported that Quinlli and Nitón are really the same thing, and, indeed, the two seemed to me to blend into a single mountain. The mountains' capacities are also blurred: Quinlli, the most versatile mountain in Salasaca, can grant weaving and other skills, and Nitón can grant other favors, such as increased fertility. Nonetheless, since Nitón specializes in improving weaving and writing skills, it remains my focus here. For analysis of Quinlli, Nitón, and other Salasaca mountains and their powers, see Corr (2000:83–133).

4. Although I didn't see any musical instruments, I heard miniature ones are sometimes left to improve musical talents.

5. See Sutton (2001:125–158) for an excellent discussion of "practical knowledge" in cooking practices, and how these may differ when written recipes are used. Other Andean anthropologists note similar weaving-writing comparisons, though with different emphases. Catherine Allen, for example, describes Peruvian women who pray to a mountain spirit and Catholic figure and say that "as they weave, their hands 'learn' from the mamacha, and they depart more accomplished in their craft" (Allen 1997:74). Allen (ibid.) next notes that pieces of paper are inserted in the same shrine, expressing material desires. This might suggest a comparison between weaving and writing, but, if so, not as similar skills (apparently the papers were not used to ask for greater writing skills); Allen also says she "will not explore the pilgrim's use of writing in any depth" (ibid.). Denise Arnold (1997), in an essay on highland Bolivia, focuses directly on weaving-writing comparisons, but she does so in terms of gender differences and patterns that differ from those of Salasaca; because Salasaca boys and girls attend school (and thus acquire writing) in almost equal numbers, and men are more involved than women in commercial weaving, I did not find gender differences highlighted in weaving-writing comparisons.

6. Other stories include the one about the man who didn't respect his parents and turned into a dog; others are reprinted in edited volumes (Athena et al. [eds.] 1975; Jara [ed.] 1987:19–20, 124–125).

7. The Costales, for example, could only say that "The deer, or horned *Purum Taruga*, of the cold jungles of Mount Teligote, comes up fully in Salasaca mythology, including the designs or artistic creations of ornamental objects, such as *chumbis* and the pants embroidery" (1959:28); but they never specified any such mythology (apart from the weavings themselves) in their chapter devoted to Salasaca "myths and stories." See also Hoffmeyer (1985:345–351). In the weaving pamphlet, I summarized Alonso's stories about the deer as follows:

> The deer is especially important for its use in medicinal remedies prepared by shamans. For example, when someone loses their senses or suffers from severe emotional upset, the best cure is a drink made from the ground-up dust of a deer's horn. Many times these illnesses are caused by a devil-like spirit who is over 6 feet tall, lives in tall trees, ravines, and abandoned houses, and who usually attacks people at night. One of the only ways to protect yourself against this spirit is to carry a club made of deer's paw.

8. Alonso's entire repertoire includes the following animal figures: deer, goat, mule, horse, worm, monkey, frog, fish, dog, duck, hen, turtle, flying squirrel, snake, giraffe, peacock, and sparrow hawk. The human figures include a mother holding up her child to see the entertainment at a fiesta, a man playing flute and drum (musical accompaniment to many fiestas), and a traditional dancer at a Corpus Christi fiesta. Other figures that do not fit the above categories are twins, the star, cross, and an olive tree branch.

9. This discussion does not apply to tapestries, which are woven on a different loom with designs dictated more by tourist tastes (hence the appearance of Zuni designs). Hoffmeyer (1985), on the other hand, has argued that the Salasaca *chumbi* designs are actually subject to radical change. Collecting and surveying many Salasaca *chumbis*, Hoffmeyer found a great variety of designs, and he claimed that few of the oldest *chumbi* designs were being reproduced by contemporary weavers (Hoffmeyer 1985:340). Part of the discrepancy here seems to result from the fact that what Hoffmeyer calls distinct designs would be deemed mere variations on the same design according to the Salasacas. Hoffmeyer simply says

that there are "hundreds of different designs and interpretations" *(cientos de motivos e interpretaciones diferentes)*, without making any distinction between these two categories. Furthermore, in an appendix with illustrations of seventy-one "designs" from *chumbis* and other weaving, he gives separate listings for many illustrations that clearly depict a single animal or theme. For example, illustrations numbered 1 through 12 all depict a deer (as Hoffmeyer himself notes in his list of the "designs"), yet they exhibit only slight differences in interpretation. Most of these different depictions would be interpreted as a single design by the Salasacas. Hoffmeyer is correct, however, in stating that some degree of change has been occurring.

10. Rappaport and Cummins describe this equation as follows:

> The Andean sense of intimacy between object and person generated by this form of recording knowledge also provides a means by which the written European text could be accommodated to Andean sensibilities. A document in this context is not regarded as generic but as specific, and literacy is not a prerequisite for its possession. If the document has been read or its contents explained, then it would continue to signify, not as a written text, but as a visual one which, like a *quipu*, communicates by its form and design information that is already known. [Rappaport and Cummins 1994:100]

11. The schools in the town center, where I made most of my observations, are run by the nuns under joint parochial-state education *(educación fisco-misional)*, but their methods of instruction resemble those of state education *(educación fiscal)*; with the exception of religious courses, they use the Ministry of Education's standardized curriculum, and most of the teachers are non-clergy (almost all whites, with a greater percentage of female teachers).

12. See Abercrombie (1998); Cummins (1994); Mignolo (1995); Rappaport (1994a); and Rappaport and Cummins (1994). As Mignolo states, "It was the belief in the accurate preservation of memory and the glorification of the past by means of alphabetic writing that resulted in a powerful complicity between the power of the letter and the authority of history" (1995:128–129).

13. In the tourists' defense, for example, it could be noted that rather than ex-
    tirpating indigenous graphic systems, they seek to celebrate and preserve
    them, at least insofar as purchasing and learning about textiles allows
    them to do so. I try to concentrate in this chapter on attitudes toward writ-
    ing per se, rather than the many complex pros and cons of tourism in gen-
    eral. See Crick (1989) for a review of the anthropology of tourism and
    Meisch (2002) for an incisive account of tourism in Otavalo (another
    highland Ecuadorian village) and images of the timeless "Noble Savage."

14. Deborah Gewertz and Frederick Errington suspect that the director of
    "Cannibal Tours" "was somewhat selective in choosing footage" (Gewertz
    and Errington 1991:220, note 6).

15. I don't use the word "tourist" in a pejorative sense here, though it is
    sometimes taken that way. I note below that distinctions should be made
    among different types of tourists, but, reluctant to proliferate terms or
    reify distinctions, I only use the term "tourist," which, unless otherwise
    specified, refers to visitors to Alonso's house, not the buyers and sellers in
    the United States.

16. This validation effect is similar to that described by Deborah Gewertz and
    Frederick Errington, who were asked by their Papua New Guinean hosts
    to write letters, type histories, and substantiate claims to power, or, as the
    authors put it, "to inscribe and thus memorialize, in effect, to make tangi-
    ble and substantial, individual lives and accomplishments" (Gewertz and
    Errington 1991:149).

17. Quoted in Sutton (2001:155). See Sutton (2001:141–158) for a full dis-
    cussion of this symbolism and variations on it in "nostalgia cookbooks,"
    with analysis of memory practices, authenticity, and commodification.

18. Admiration for Alonso's father's weaving was shared by the two anthro-
    pologists who first investigated his work, Lynn Meisch and Laura Miller.
    One of the belts they collected from Alonso's father appears in the Textile
    Museum in Washington, D.C., and photos of the belt (and Alonso and his
    family) appear in an accompanying book, together with a text that states
    "Salasaca belts are among the finest in Ecuador" (Miller 1998:131).
    Alonso's business is an example of what Erik Cohen (2000: 250) calls "re-
    habilitative commercialization of ethnic crafts."

19. For more information about how to visit, you can contact Alonso by email
    at alonsopilla@hotmail.com (he usually gets his email when visiting the

Monday market in Ambato) or by calling him at (011) 593-99840-125. For an account of folklore music in Otavalo, see Meisch (2002).

20. For an Ecuadorian example, see Belote and Belote (1981:470–471).

21. Other works include the following: Abercrombie (1998); Boone and Mignolo (eds.) (1994); Campbell (1995:157–165); Gebhart-Sayer (1985); Gow (1990); Gruzinski (1993); Guevara-Gil and Salomon (1994); Guss (1986); Harris (1995); Hill and Wright (1988); Howe (1979); Jaye and Mitchell (eds.) (1999); Orlove (1991); Ortiz Rescaniere (1973); Perrin (1985); Platt (1992); Pollock (1993:185–187); Ramón Valarezo (1991); Sánchez Parga (1983); and Skar (1994).

7

Conclusion

"Dreams—We have no dreams at all or interesting ones. We should learn to be awake in the same way— not at all or in an interesting manner."

—Friedrich Nietzsche, *The Gay Science*

Anthropologists often promise to make the strange familiar and the familiar strange, but nobody has done this better than Gabriel García Márquez, the master of magical-realist fiction. In *One Hundred Years of Solitude*, García Márquez describes a town suffering from insomnia and amnesia, and he explains that the town leader, desperately fighting rapid memory loss, took an ink brush and "marked everything with its name: *table, chair, clock, door, wall, bed, pan.* He went to the corral and marked the animals and plants: *cow, goat, pig, hen, cassava, caladium, banana*" (García Márquez 1971:53). The leader soon realized that people might need to be reminded how to use things as well, so he posted explicit instructions throughout the town, such as a sign hung from the neck of a cow that stated, "*This is the cow. She must be milked every morning so that she will produce milk, and the milk must be boiled in order to be mixed with coffee to make coffee and milk*" (ibid.).

This scene is an elaborate joke. The labeling scheme has obviously reached comically absurd proportions, even if the humor in explaining that you mix coffee and milk to make "coffee and milk" (café con leche) inevitably comes through better in the Spanish original than the English translation. What is perhaps less obvious is that the joke is on state regulation, the state's use of archival documents to record, name, classify, and control its citizens. Of course, as a parody, the scene exaggerates these state practices—but only slightly. I saw stickers on doors throughout Ecuador indicating that the household, including cows and other animals, had been counted in the 2001 national census. And such regulation is not limited to Latin America. As a Welsh farmer recently complained about European Union regulation of cattle movement and other agricultural practices, "It's got dreadful with forms now" (Jones 2000:71). For taxation and other purposes, the state *does* go into the corral and mark the animals and plants, and it even attaches signs to cows that virtually say, "This is a cow." Such recording of blatantly obvious information—the fact that this animal is a chicken, this person is a farmer—is an inherent aspect of all state bureaucracy. Employing the necessary degree of exaggeration, García Márquez highlights these classification routines in his novel.[1]

On another level, the insomnia scene pokes fun at people whose memories are weakened by reliance on written mnemonics—people who cannot remember a telephone number because they just wrote it down. García Márquez is partly echoing Plato, who feared that writing would "produce forgetfulness in the souls of those who have learned it, through lack of practice at using their memory" (Rowe 1988:123).[2] But whereas Plato was worried about writing's effects on dialogical knowledge, García Márquez uses individual memory loss as a symbol for the loss of indigenous cultural memory. Thus, a Guajiro Indian woman first recognizes and explains to the others the truly devastating effect of the plague of insomnia: "a kind of idiocy that had no past" (1971[1967]:50). And while Plato was speaking shortly after the invention of alphabetic writing, when there still seemed to be a chance of limiting its effects (Gee 1988), García Márquez is speaking to readers who, as the heirs to more than two millennia of writing's ascendance in daily life, commonly assume that writing is practical, rational, and superior to oral memory.

García Márquez's scene inverts those assumptions, making writing a surprising object of curiosity. The author refers to the labeling scheme as "the spell of an imaginary reality, one invented by themselves, which was less practical for them but more comforting" (García Márquez 1971:53). The true magic, it turns out, is archival writing.

The "plague of insomnia" scene illustrates the way writing can seem strange when looked at from alternative angles. And this scene is not an isolated moment in Latin American literature: Roberto González Echevarría (1990) argues to good effect that Latin American fiction of the past several centuries has been modeled on images of legal and scientific archives.[3] The "plague of insomnia" scene can stand, then, for the centrality of archival imagery within Latin American literature. But where literary analysis leaves off, ethnographic investigation begins. Obviously indigenous cultures did not die when they first encountered alphabetic writing, nor were their cultural memories wiped clean by colonialism, as harsh as it was; in contemporary Latin America and elsewhere, indigenous cultures are alive and well, despite centuries of contact with documentation. For that matter, archival documents have been the focus of interactions with bureaucratic authorities in the modern era for *all* non-elite peoples, indigenous and otherwise, given the ubiquity of the archival writing that accompanies the nation-state, religions of the book, and capitalism. Thus, the interesting question is: What do specific communities make of bureaucratic archives? Put differently, how did they respond when the "plague of insomnia" reached their towns? This is the question addressed in the preceding pages.

One of the answers to emerge in the Salasaca case is that non-elites themselves grasp the intimate relationship between archives and power. The Salasacas consistently use archival writing as a concrete representation of church and state power, specifically the relationship between state documentation and identity conceptions postulated by previous research (Cohn 1990; Corrigan and Sayer 1985; Kertzer and Arel [eds.] 2002; Scott 1988). A benefit of ethnographic study of literacy (Rappaport 1994a–c; Street 1984), then, is to reveal the way social-science theories get confirmed and replicated in local views. Another benefit is seeing the way literacy symbolism is employed in struggles with church and state power, demonstrating that the purview of resistance studies (Scott 1985, 1990) has to be expanded to include writing symbolism, rather than just oral expressions. More generally, investigating writing symbolism offers insight into state-local relations and conceptions of power, whether such conceptions take the form of resistance or not (Anderson 1990; Geertz 1980). To understand what people think of power, we have to find out what they think about archival writing.

Although the ethnographic focus here has been a single Latin American community, the underlying conceptualization of literacy, memory, and power can clearly bring about a re-evaluation of entire theories. Benedict Anderson's *Imagined Communities* (1991[1983]), for example, looks different when viewed from the perspective advocated here. In explaining print's effects on the creation of national identities, Anderson points out that, in early modern European history, printed products created a new sense of language permanence, which was useful to celebrations of national languages: "print-capitalism gave a new fixity to language, which in the long run helped to build that image of antiquity so central to the subjective idea of the nation. . . . [T]he printed book kept a permanent form, capable of virtually infinite reproduction, temporally and spatially" (Anderson 1991[1983]:44). As plausible as this idea is, especially to contemporary Europeans and North Americans accustomed to viewing print as more permanent than speaking, it neglects cultural influences over conceptions of language "fixity." There is no such thing as a neutral, objective measure of language permanence, only cultural notions that make it appear so. Individual cultures have varying definitions of language permanence, and they do not necessarily privilege language stability or print over oral memory. It makes all the difference when these definitions are seen as cultural constructions, rather than inherent aspects of print. From this perspective, the interesting question is not how print transformed national consciousness, but how these transformations went hand in hand with culturally specific conceptions of print itself (Silverstein 1999; Wogan 2001).

This alternative perspective on language permanence has already been suggested by the previous discussion of Salasaca writing-and-weaving comparisons, but a glance at Latin American graffiti makes this case more fully, and, moreover, indicates that a cultural perspective on archival literacy can explain more than magical beliefs in rural communities. Given that urban graffiti in Latin America (and elsewhere) is characterized by its transience (Silva 1986), one could argue that its very form provides a sardonic commentary on the ideology of archival literacy, which holds that writing is more permanent than human memory. While Anderson and others celebrate the permanence of books, graffiti aims for another kind of language fixity: the staying power in individual memory of a soulful message. Graffiti is more akin to aphorisms, as described by a notorious master of the form, Friedrich Nietzsche: "He who writes in blood and aphorisms does not want to be read, he wants to be learned by heart" (1961[1883]:67).

Ecuadorian urban graffiti, in particular, shares this aphoristic quality. Rather than just saying "Kilroy was here," this graffiti pulses with poetic and philosophical overtones. Walking along busy streets in Quito and Ambato, I have been taken aback by messages like "Let me walk along the edges of your mind," "Mine is a free life but at times I feel alone," and "The end of dreams is the dream of the system" (see Figure 7.1).

Figure 7.1   *Quito graffiti: "The end of dreams is the dream of the system."*

This is writing not meant to enter the archives but to penetrate and reside in the soul, even to be learned by heart. Interviews with young Quito graffiti writers give some sense of these motivations:

> Q: *What is graffiti for you?*
> A: *It's a medium of communication and an art. We believe that it's a tie that you can put around other people. We seek a way not to be isolated islands in the world; that way is our graffiti.*
> Q: *Do you think people understand your graffiti?*
> A: *We don't know, but the important thing is that you say what you think, and if just one person understands your message, it was worth creating it.*
> Q: *Why do you use a tearful eye as the mark of your group?*
> A: *Because when you cry, you unload yourself; when you make graffiti, you scream at the people what you feel, and that frees you. When there's a profound feeling of happiness and sadness, you cry; it's a nectar of sensitivity.* [Alex 1994:142]

Another graffiti writer puts it this way, with characteristic wit: "Galileo said it right: 'You write for friends who are far away.' And I write for my friends. If they now read others' graffiti, that's not my fault" (Alex 1994:140).

Such graffiti has a dual status: it is public writing, like state documentation, yet unlike such documentation, it lacks archival permanence and is meant to burn itself into individual memory. Like Nietzsche's epigraph ("epigraffiti"?) and the dream imagery in Figure 7.1, graffiti even blurs the lines between unconsciousness and consciousness, night and day: it gets written in the dark hours of the night, so that it can be read in the light of day. Such writing is a public dream: an outward expression of inner sentiments, reveries, and ruminations. Graffiti artists' acts of vandalism (and resistance) also transform private property into public space: a previously unnoticed wall in front of someone's house suddenly becomes a provocative billboard message calling out to passersby. As writing that is both permanent and ephemeral, public and private, graffiti reverses and parodies the conventional relationship between archives and memory in a García Márquez scene writ large—or at least this is one interpretation worth considering. The graffiti example suggests, if nothing else, the possibilities for looking at various forms of writing in terms of their relationship to archives, the state, and memory.

Research could take many other directions. It would be interesting to know, for example, what it says about Thai attitudes toward print and power when monks ward off evil by tapping the heads of worshippers with rolled-up newspapers (Wongpaithoon 1996). Or can any commentary on power be gleaned from the way indigenous Peruvians wrap sacred offerings in white paper and leave written requests for mountain spirits during pilgrimages (Allen 1988:153–156, 197; 1997)?

Such questions will be worth asking as long as power inequalities exist and get exercised through writing—in other words, for the indefinite future. And research possibilities are hardly limited to Third World communities. We can ultimately follow García Márquez in looking at literacy as one of the central myths of European/North American society, turning "the object of attention away from myth as an expression of so-called primitive cultures to the myths of modern society: the book, writing, reading, instruments of a quest for self-knowledge that lie beyond the solace mythic interpretations of the world usually afford" (González Echevarría 1990:29). Taking this tack disrupts anthropology's traditional identity as the study of unconscious orality in non-Western societies (Certeau 1988) and shows that magic and myth abound at all levels.

Notes

1. Reflecting the role of the state, the one who imposes the labeling scheme is José Arcadio Buendía, a state figure who has recently determined the layout of the town's streets and houses, distributed land, and organized commerce (García Márquez 1971[1967]:44–45). The town's evolution at this point parallels the late colonial period in Latin American history: hence the newly independent, more active state arrives at this same time in the figure of the Magistrate, who, authorized by an "official document" from the government, writes an order to have all houses painted blue and white for national independence. José Arcadio Buendía initially resents ceding authority to the Magistrate's written orders, but the two men's families soon become intertwined through intermarriage (García Márquez 1971[1967]:61).

2. With multiple levels of voicing, Plato is quoting Socrates, who is supposed to be quoting King Thamus. See Gee (1988) for an excellent discussion of Plato's *Phaedrus* and its relationship to modern literacy theories.

3. Although my analysis obviously accords with González Echevarría's emphasis on archives, his own interpretation of *One Hundred Years of Solitude* does not focus on the "plague of insomnia," but, rather, the gypsy Melquíades' undeciphered manuscripts. See Rappaport (1992) for an excellent discussion of González Echevarría's book; and, for another important study of the nexus of elite culture, literature, and state power in Latin America, see Angel Rama's work (1984) on the "lettered city."

References

Abercrombie, Thomas. 1991. To Be Indian, to Be Bolivian: "Ethnic" and "National" Discourses of Identity. In *Nation-States and Indians in Latin America*. Greg Urban and Joel Sherzer, eds. Pp. 95–130. Austin: University of Texas Press.

_____. 1998. *Pathways of Memory and Power: Ethnography and History Among an Andean People*. Madison: University of Wisconsin Press.

Abu-Lughod, Lila. 1990. The Romance of Resistance: Tracing Transformations of Power Through Bedouin Women. *American Ethnologist* 17:41–55.

Adorno, Rolena, ed. 1982. *From Oral to Written Expression: Native Andean Chronicles of the Early Colonial Period*. Syracuse: Maxwell School of Citizenship and Public Affairs.

Ahearn, Laura M. 2001. *Invitations to Love: Literacy, Love Letters, and Social Change in Nepal*. Ann Arbor: University of Michigan Press.

Albornoz Peralta, Oswaldo. 1971. *Las luchas indígenas en el Ecuador*. Guayaquil: Editorial Claridad.

Alex, Ron. 1994. *Quito: Una ciudad de grafitis*. Quito: Editora Luz de América.

Allen, Catherine J. 1988. *The Hold Life Has: Coca and Cultural Identity in an Andean Community*. Washington, DC: Smithsonian Institution Press.

_____. 1997. When Pebbles Move Mountains: Iconicity and Symbolism in Quechua Ritual. In *Creating Context in Andean Cultures*. Rosaleen Howard-Malverde, ed. Pp. 73–84. Oxford: Oxford University Press.

Anderson, Benedict R. O'G. 1990. *Language and Power: Exploring Political Cultures in Indonesia*. Ithaca: Cornell University Press.

_____. 1991 [1983]. *Imagined Communities: Reflections on the Origin and Spread of Nationalism*. 2nd edition. London: Verso.

Appadurai, Arjun. 1993. Number in the Colonial Imagination. In *Orientalism and the Postcolonial Predicament: Perspectives on South Asia*. Carole A. Breckenridge and Peter van der Veer, eds. Pp. 314–339. Philadelphia: University of Pennsylvania Press.

Arias, Juan Felix. 1994. *Historia de una esperanza: Los Apoderados Espiritualistas de Chuquisaca, 1936–1964*. La Paz: Ediciones Aruwiyiri.

Arnold, Denise. 1997. Making Men in Her Own Image: Gender, Text, and Textile in Qaqachaka. In *Creating Context in Andean Cultures*. Rosaleen Howard-Malverde, ed. Pp. 99–134. Oxford: Oxford University Press.

_____, ed. 1997. *Más allá del silencio: las fronteras de género en los Andes*. La Paz: CIASE/ILCA.

Arnove, Robert F., and Harvey J. Graff. 1987. Introduction. In *National Literacy Campaigns: Historical and Comparative Perspectives*. Robert F. Arnove and Harvey J. Graff, eds. Pp. 1–28. New York: Plenum Press.

Athena, Olivia, Hugh Dufner, Agustín Jerez J., Monica Lyons, eds. 1975. *Urdimal Tiempomunda*. Quito: Instituto Inter-Andino de Desarrollo.

Axtell, James. 1988. *After Columbus: Essays in the Ethnohistory of Colonial North America*. Oxford: Oxford University Press.

Barton, David, and Mary Hamilton. 1988. *Local Literacies: Reading and Writing in One Community*. London: Routledge.

_____, eds. 1994. *Worlds of Literacy*. Clevedon: Multilingual Matters.

Bastien, Joseph W. 1978. *Mountain of the Condor: Metaphor and Ritual in an Andean Ayllu*. Prospect Heights, IL: Waveland Press.

_____. 1985. Qollahuaya-Andean Body Concepts: A Topographical-Hydraulic Model of Physiology. *American Anthropologist* 87:595–611.

_____. 1989. Differences Between Kallawaya-Andean and Greek-European Humoral Theory. *Social Science and Medicine* 28:45–51.

Behar, Ruth. 1993. *Translated Woman: Crossing the Border with Esperanza's Story*. Boston: Beacon Press.

Belote, Jim, and Linda Smith Belote. 1977a. The Limitation of Obligation in Saraguro Kinship. In *Andean Kinship and Marriage*. Ralph Bolton and Enrique Mayer, eds. Pp. 106–116. Washington, DC: American Anthropological Association.

_____. 1977b. El sistema de cargos de fiestas en Saraguro. In *Temas sobre la continuidad y adaptación cultural ecuatoriana*. Marcelo F. Naranjo, ed. Pp. 47–73. Quito: Universidad Católica del Ecuador.

Belote, Linda Smith and Tim Belote. 1981. Development in Spite of Itself: The Saraguro Case. In *Cultural Transformations and Ethnicity in Modern Ecuador*. Norman E. Whitten, Jr., ed. Pp. 450–476. Urbana: University of Illinois Press.

_____. 1984. Drain from the Bottom: Individual Ethnic Identity Change in Southern Ecuador. *Social Forces* 63:24–50.

_____. 1988. Gender, Ethnicity, and Modernization: Saraguro Women in a Changing World. In *Multidisciplinary Studies in Andean Anthropology*. J. Vitzthum, ed. Ann Arbor: Michigan Discussions in Anthropology 8:110–116.

Belote, Linda Smith. 2002. *Relaciones interétnicas en Saraguro*. Quito: Abya-Yala.

Besnier, Niko. 1995. *Literacy, Emotion, and Authority: Reading and Writing on a Polynesian Atoll*. Cambridge: Cambridge University Press.

Bledsoe, Caroline H., and Kenneth M. Robey. 1993. Arabic Literacy and Secrecy among the Mende of Sierra Leone. In *Cross-Cultural Approaches to Literacy*. Brian V. Street, ed. Pp. 110–134. Cambridge: Cambridge University Press.

Bloch, Maurice. 1993. The Uses of Schooling and Literacy in a Zafimaniry Village. In *Cross-Cultural Approaches to Literacy*. Brian V. Street, ed. Pp. 87–109. Cambridge: Cambridge University Press.

Boone, Elizabeth Hill, and Walter D. Mignolo, eds. 1994. *Writing Without Words: Alternative Literacies in Mesoamerica and the Andes.* Durham: Duke University Press.

Borchart de Moreno, Christiana. 1983. Origen y conformación de la hacienda colonial. In *Nueva historia del Ecuador: Epoca Colonial III.* Volume 5. Enrique Ayala Mora, ed. Pp. 142–166. Quito: Corporación Editora Nacional.

Borges, Jorge Luis. 1962. The Library of Babel. In *Ficciones.* Anthony Kerrigan, trans. Pp. 79–88. New York: Grove Press.

Borque, Susan C., and Kay Barbara Warren. 1981. *Women of the Andes: Patriarchy and Social Change in Two Peruvian Towns.* Ann Arbor: University of Michigan Press.

Bricker, Victoria Reifler. 1973. *Ritual Humor in Highland Chiapas.* Austin: University of Texas Press.

Brotherston, Gordon. 1981. A Controversial Guide to the Language of America, 1643. In *1642: Literature and Power in the Seventeenth Century: Proceedings of the Essex Conference on the Sociology of Literature.* Francis Barker, Jay Bernstein, John Coombes, Peter Hulme, Jennifer Stone, and Jon Stratton, eds. Pp. 84–100. Essex, UK: University of Essex Press.

Brown, Michael F. 1988. Shamanism and Its Discontents. *Medical Anthropology Quarterly* 2:102–120.

———. 1991. Beyond Resistance: A Comparative Study of Utopian Renewal in Amazonia. *Ethnohistory* 38:388–413.

———. 1996. On Resisting Resistance. *American Anthropologist* 98:729–749.

Campbell, Alan. 1995. *Getting to Know Waiwai: An Amazonian Ethnography.* New York: Routledge.

Canessa, Andrew. 2000. Fear and Loathing on the *Kharisiri* Trail: Alterity and Identity in the Andes. *Journal of the Royal Anthropological Institute* 6:705–720.

Casagrande, Joseph B. 1977. Estrategias para sobrevivir: Los indígenas de la sierra. In *Temas sobre la continuidad y adaptación cultural ecuatoriana.* Marcelo F. Naranjo, José C. Pereira V., and Norman E. Whitten, Jr., eds. Pp. 77–104. Quito: Universidad Católica del Ecuador.

Cereceda, Verónica. 1986. The Semiology of Andean Textiles: The Talegas of Isluga. In *Anthropological History of Andean Polities.* John Murra, Nathan Wachtel, and Jacques Revel, eds. Pp. 149–173. New York: Cambridge University Press.

Certeau, Michel de. 1988. *The Writing of History.* Tom Conley, trans. New York: Columbia University Press.

Cervone, Emma, and Freddy Rivera, eds. 1999. *Ecuador Racista: Imágenes e Identidades.* Quito: FLACSO.

Choque Quispe, María Eugenia. 1992. La estructura de poder en la comunidad originaria de Salasaca. M.A. thesis, Department of Andean History, Facultad Latinoamericana de Ciencias Sociales (Quito).

Clanchy, M. T. 1979. *From Memory to Written Record: England, 1066–1307.* Cambridge: Cambridge University Press.

Clifford, James. 1986. On Ethnographic Allegory. In *Writing Culture.* James Clifford and George E. Marcus, eds. Pp. 98–121. Berkeley: University of California Press.

———. 1988. *Predicament of Culture: Twentieth-Century Ethnography, Literature, and Art.* Cambridge: Harvard University Press.

Coba Robalino, José María. 1929. Monografía general del cantón Píllaro. Quito.

Cohen, Erik. 2000. Rehabilitative Commercialization: The Revival of Ban Namon Weaving. In *The Commercialized Crafts of Thailand: Hill Tribes and Lowland Villages*. Erik Cohen, ed. Pp. 250–274. Honolulu: University of Hawaii Press.

Cohn, Bernard. 1990. The Census, Social Structure and Objectification in South Asia. In *An Anthropologist among the Historians and Other Essays*. Bernard Cohn, ed. Pp. 224–254. Oxford: Oxford University Press.

_____, and Nicholas B. Dirks. 1988. Beyond the Fringe: The Nation State, Colonialism, and the Technologies of Power. *Journal of Historical Sociology* 1:224–229.

Collins, James. 1995. Literacy and Literacies. *Annual Review of Anthropology* 24:75–93.

Colloredo-Mansfield, Rudi. 1999. *The Native Leisure Class: Consumption and Cultural Creativity in the Andes*. Chicago: University of Chicago Press.

Condori Chura, Leandro, and Esteban Ticona Alejo. 1992. *El escribano de los caciques apoderados: Kasikinakan puriraunakan qillqiripa*. La Paz: Ediciones Aruwiyiri.

Corr, Rachel E. 2000. Cosmology and Personal Experience: Representations of the Sacred Landscape in Salasaca, Ecuador. Ph.D. dissertation, Department of Anthropology, University of Illinois at Urbana-Champaign.

_____. 2002. Reciprocity, Communion, and Sacrifice: Food in Andean Ritual and Social Life. *Food and Foodways* 10:1–25.

Corrigan, Philip, and Derek Sayer. 1985. *The Great Arch: English State Formation as Cultural Revolution*. Oxford: Basil Blackwell.

Costales Samaniego, Alfredo, and Piedad Peñaherrera. 1959. *Los Salasacas*. Quito: Sección de Antropología Social del Instituto Ecuatoriano de Antropología.

Crick, Malcolm. 1989. Representations of International Tourism in the Social Sciences: Sun, Sex, Sights, Savings, and Servility. *Annual Review of Anthropology* 18:307–344.

Cummins, Thomas B. F. 1994. Representation in the Sixteenth Century and the Colonial Image of the Inca. In *Writing Without Words: Alternative Literacies in Mesoamerica and the Andes*. Elizabeth Hill Boone and Walter D. Mignolo, eds. Pp. 188–219. Durham: Duke University Press.

Dash, Robert, ed. 1997. Ecuador, Part I: Politics and Rural Issues. Special Issue of *Latin American Perspectives* 24:3–103.

De Soto, Hernando. 2000. *The Mystery of Capital: Why Capitalism Triumphs in the West and Fails Everywhere Else*. New York: Basic Books.

Ehrenreich, Jeffrey. 1985. Isolation, Retreat and Secrecy: Dissembling Behavior among the Coaiquer Indians. In *Political Anthropology in Ecuador: Perspectives from Indigenous Cultures*. Jeffrey Ehrenreich, ed. Pp. 25–58. Albany, NY: Society for Latin American Anthropology.

Evans-Pritchard, E. E. 1976 [1937]. *Witchcraft, Oracles, and Magic among the Azande*. Oxford: Clarendon Press.

Fischer, Edward F., and R. McKenna Brown, eds. 1996. *Maya Cultural Activism in Guatemala*. Austin: University of Texas Press.

Flores Freire, Fanny. 1987. Organización administrativa del Registro Civil en la provincia del Tungurahua. Thesis, Facultad de Ciencias Administrativas, Universidad Técnica de Ambato.

Foster, George M. 1953. Relationships Between Spanish and Spanish-American Folk Medicine. *Journal of American Folklore* 66:2001–217.

_____. 1994. *Hippocrates' Latin American Legacy: Humoral Medicine in the New World.* Langhorne, PA: Gordon and Breach.

Foster, Robert J. 1991. Making National Cultures in the Global Ecumene. *Annual Review of Anthropology* 20:235–260.

_____. 2002. *Materializing the Nation: Commodities, Consumption, and Media in Papua New Guinea.* Bloomington: Indiana University Press.

Foucault, Michel. 1977. *Discipline and Punish: The Birth of the Prison.* Alan Sheridan, trans. New York: Pantheon.

Fox, Richard G., and Orin Starn, eds. 1997. *Between Resistance and Revolution: Cultural Politics and Social Protest.* New Brunswick, NJ: Rutgers University Press.

Fuentealba M., Gerardo. 1983. La sociedad indígena en las primeras décadas de la República: Continuidades coloniales y cambios republicanos. In *Nueva historia del Ecuador: Epoca Republicana III*. Volume 8. Enrique Ayala Mora, ed. Pp. 47–73. Quito: Corporación Editora Nacional.

Fuentes Roldán, Alfredo. 1969. "Finados" en Calderón, Provincia de Pichincha. *Revista del Folklore Ecuatoriano* 3:155–174.

García Márquez, Gabriel. 1971. *One Hundred Years of Solitude.* Gregory Rabassa, trans. New York: Avon Books.

Gebhart-Sayer, Angelika. 1985. The Geometric Designs of the Shipibo-Conibo in Ritual Context. *Journal of Latin American Lore* 11:143–175.

Gee, James Paul. 1986. Orality and Literacy: From The Savage Mind to Ways with Words. *TESOL Quarterly* 20:719–746.

_____. 1988. The Legacies of Literacy: From Plato to Freire Through Harvey Graff. *Harvard Educational Review* 58:195–212.

_____. 1996 [1990]. *Social Linguistics and Literacies: Ideology in Discourses.* 2nd edition. London: Taylor and Francis.

Geertz, Clifford. 1980. *Negara: The Theatre State in Nineteenth-Century Bali.* Princeton: Princeton University Press.

Gelb, I. J. 1963 [1952]. *A Study of Writing.* 2nd edition. Chicago: University of Chicago Press.

Gelles, Paul, Gabriela, Martínez Escobar, Ricardo, Valderrama Fernández, and Carmen Escalante Gutiérrez. 1996. *Andean Lives: Gregorio Condori Mamani and Asunta Quispe Huamán.* Austin: University of Texas Press.

Gewertz, Deborah, and Fredrick Errington. 1991. *Twisted Histories, Altered Contexts: Representing the Chambri in a World System.* Cambridge: Cambridge University Press.

González Echevarría, Roberto. 1990. *Myth and Archive: A Theory of Latin American Identity.* Cambridge: Cambridge University Press.

Goody, Jack. 1977. *The Domestication of the Savage Mind.* Cambridge: Cambridge University Press.

_____. 1987. *Interface Between the Written and the Oral.* Cambridge: Cambridge University Press.

_____. 2000. *The Power of the Written Tradition.* Washington: Smithsonian Institution Press.

Gose, Peter. 1994. *Deathly Waters and Hungry Mountains: Agrarian Ritual and Class Formation in an Andean Town.* Toronto: University of Toronto Press.

Gow, Peter. 1990. Could Sangama Read? The Origin of Writing among the Piro of Eastern Peru. *History and Anthropology* 5:87–103.

Graff, Harvey. 1979. *The Literacy Myth: Literacy and Social Structure in the Nineteenth-Century City.* New York: Academic Press.

Gregory, C. 1986. On Taussig on Aristotle and Chevalier on Everyone. *Social Analysis* 19:64–69.

Gross, Daniel R. 1983. Fetishism and Functionalism: The Political Economy of Capitalist Development in Latin America: A Review Article. *Comparative Studies in Society and History* 25:694–702.

Gruzinski, Serge. 1993. *The Conquest of Mexico: The Incorporation of Indian Societies into the Western World, 16th–18th Centuries.* Eileen Corrigan, trans. Cambridge: Polity Press.

Guerrero, Andrés. 1994. Una imagen ventrílocua: El discurso liberal de la "desgraciada raza indígena" a fines del siglo XIX. In *Imagenes e imagineros: Representaciones de los indígenas ecuatorianos, siglos XIX y XX.* Blanca Muratorio, ed. Pp. 197–254. Quito: FLACSO.

Guevara, Darío. 1945. *Puerta de El Dorado, Monografía del Cantón Pelileo.* Quito: Editora Moderna.

Guevara, Moposita et al. 1992. Aproximaciones Etimológicas y Críticas en Torno a la Onomástica Antroponímica de los Salasacas. B.A. Thesis, Facultad de Ciencias de la Educación, Universidad Técnica de Ambato, Ambato, Ecuador.

Guevara-Gil, Armando, and Frank Salomon. 1994. A "Personal Visit": Colonial Political Ritual and the Making of the Indians of the Andes. *Colonial Latin American Review* 3:3–36.

Guss, David M. 1986. Keeping It Oral: A Yekuana Ethnology. *American Ethnologist* 13:413–429.

_____. 1996. Reading the Mesa: An Interview with Eduardo Calderón. In *The Book, Spiritual Instrument.* Jerome Rothenberg and David Guss, eds. Pp. 45–52. New York: Granary Books.

_____. 2000. *The Festive State: Race, Ethnicity, and Nationalism as Cultural Performance.* Berkeley: University of California Press.

Hamilton, Sarah. 1998. *The Two-Headed Household: Gender and Rural Development in the Ecuadorean Andes.* Pittsburgh: University of Pittsburgh Press.

Harbsmeier, Michael. 1985. Early Travels to Europe: Some Remarks on the Magic of Writing. In *Europe and Its Other.* Francis Barker, Peter Hulme, Margaret Iverson, and Diana Loxley, eds. Pp. 72–87. Essex: University of Essex Press.

_____. 1988. Inventions of Writing. In *State and Society: The Emergence and Development of Social Hierarchy and Political Centralization.* John Gledhill,

Barbara Bender, and Mogens Trolle Larsen, eds. Pp. 253–276. London: Unwin Hyman.

Harris, Olivia. 1978. Complementarity and Conflict: An Andean View of Women and Men. In *Sex and Age as Principles of Social Differentiation.* J. S. LaFontaine, ed. Pp. 21–40. London: Academic Press.

Harrison, Regina. 1989. *Signs, Songs, and Memory in the Andes: Translating Quechua Language and Culture.* Austin: University of Texas Press.

Hartmann, Roswith. 1973. Conmemoración de muertos en la Sierra ecuatoriana. *Indiana* (Berlin) 1:179–189.

Heath, Shirley Brice. 1983. *Ways with Words: Life and Work in Communities and Classrooms.* Cambridge: Cambridge University Press.

Herzfeld, Michael. 1987. *Anthropology Through the Looking-Glass: Critical Ethnography in the Margins of Europe.* Cambridge: Cambridge University Press.

_____. 1992. *The Social Production of Indifference: Exploring the Symbolic Roots of Western Bureaucracy.* New York: Berg.

Hess, Carmen. 1997. *Hungry for Hope: On the Cultural and Communicative Dimensions of Development in Highland Ecuador.* New York: Stylus.

Hill, Jonathan D. 1996. *History, Power, Identity: Ethnogenesis in the Americas, 1492–1992.* Iowa City: University of Iowa Press.

_____, ed. 1987. *Rethinking History and Myth: Indigenous South American Perspectives on the Past.* Urbana: University of Illinois Press.

_____, and Robin M. Wright. 1988. Time, Narrative, and Ritual: Historical Interpretations from an Amazonian Society. In *Rethinking History and Myth: Indigenous South American Perspectives on the Past.* Jonathan D. Hill, ed. Pp. 78–105. Urbana: University of Illinois Press.

Hirschkind, Lynn. 1995. History of the Indian Population of Cañar. *Colonial Latin American Historical Review* 4:311–342.

Hirschman, Charles. 1987. The Meaning and Measurement of Ethnicity in Malaysia: An Analysis of Census Classifications. *Journal of Asian Studies* 46:555–582.

Hoffmeyer, Hans. 1985. Diseños Salasacas. *Cultura: Revista del Banco Central del Ecuador* 7:339–371.

Hornberger, Nancy H., ed. 1997. *Indigenous Literacies in the Americas: Language Planning from the Bottom Up.* New York: Mouton de Gruyter.

Howe, James. 1979. The Effects of Writing on the Cuna Political System. *Ethnology* 28:1–17.

Hugh-Jones, Stephen. 1989. Waríbi and the White Men: History and Myth in Northwest Amazonia. In *History and Ethnicity.* Elizabeth Tonkin, Maryon McDonald, and Malcolm Chapman, eds. Pp. 53–70. London: Routledge.

Instituto Nacional de Estadística y Censos. 1991. *V Censo de Población y IV de Vivienda 1990: Resultados Definitivos.* Tomo I-II. Quito: Instituto Nacional de Estadística y Censos.

Irvine, Judith. 1992. Ideologies of Honorific Language. *Pragmatics* 2:251–262.

Isbell, Billie Jean. 1978. *To Defend Ourselves: Ecology and Ritual in an Andean Village.* Austin: Institute of Latin American Studies.

Israel, J. I. 1975. *Class and Politics in Colonial Mexico, 1610–1670*. London: Oxford Historical Monographs.

Jackson, Jean E. 1995. "Déjà Endtendu": The Liminal Qualities of Anthropological Fieldnotes. In *Representation in Ethnography*. John Van Maanen, ed. Pp. 36–78. London: Sage.

Jara, Fausto, ed. 1987 [1982]. *Taruca, Ecuador Quichuacunapac rimashca rimai cuna, La venada, Literatura oral Quichua del Ecuador*. Ruth Moya, trans. Quito: Abya Yala.

Jaye, Barbara H., and William P. Mitchell, eds. 1999. *Picturing Faith: A Facsimile Edition of the Pictographic Quechua Catechism in the Huntington Free Library*. Bronx: Huntington Free Library.

Jones, Kathryn. 2000. Becoming Just Another Alphanumeric Code: Farmers' Encounters with the Literacy and Discourse Practices of Agricultural Bureaucracy at the Livestock Auction. In *Situated Literacies*. David Barton, Mary Barton, and Roz Ivanic, eds. Pp. 70–90. London: Routledge.

Joralemon, Donald, and Douglas Sharon. 1993. *Sorcery and Shamanism: Curanderos and Clients in Northern Peru*. Salt Lake City: University of Utah Press.

Kalman, Judy. 1999. *Writing on the Plaza: Mediated Literacy Practice Among Scribes and Clients in Mexico City*. Cresskill, NJ: Hampton Press.

Kaplan, Martha, and John D. Kelly. Rethinking Resistance: Dialogics of "Disaffection" in Colonial Fiji. *American Ethnologist* 21:123–151.

Keller-Cohen, Deborah. 1993. The Web of Literacy: Speaking, Reading and Writing in 17th and 18th Century America. In *Literacy: Interdisciplinary Conversations*. Deborah Keller-Cohen, ed. Pp. 155–176. Creskill, NJ: Hampton Press.

Kertzer, David I., and Dominique Arel. 2002. Censuses, Identity Formation, and the Struggle for Political Power. In *Census and Identity: The Politics of Race, Ethnicity, and Language in National Censuses*. David I. Kertzer and Dominique Arel, eds. Pp. 1–42. Cambridge: Cambridge University Press.

_____, eds. 2002. *Census and Identity: The Politics of Race, Ethnicity, and Language in National Censuses*. Cambridge: Cambridge University Press.

Kuhn, Thomas S. 1971 [1962]. *The Structure of Scientific Revolutions*. 2nd edition. Chicago: University of Chicago Press.

Kulick, Don, and Christopher Stroud. 1990. Christianity, Cargo and Ideas of Self: Patterns of Literacy in a Papua New Guinean Village. *Man* 25:286–304.

Lakoff, George. 1995. Metaphor, Morality, and Politics, Or, Why Conservatives Have Left Liberals in the Dust. *Social Research* 62:177–214.

Larrea Cabrera, Gustavo. 1990. *Sociología de la educación: hacía una nueva educación*. Quito: Abya Yala.

Lévi-Strauss, Claude. 1981. *Tristes Tropiques*. John and Doreen Weightman, trans. New York: Atheneum.

López Austin, Alfredo. 1980. *Cuerpo humano e ideología: Las concepciones de los antiguos nahuas*. Mexico: UNAM.

Lyons, Barry. 1999. "Taita Chimborazo and Mama Tungurahua": A Quichua Song, A Fieldwork Story. *Anthropology and Humanism* 24:32–46.

MacCannell, Dean. 1992. *Empty Meeting Grounds: The Tourist Papers*. London: Routledge.

MacCormack, Sabine. 1991. *Religion in the Andes: Vision and Imagination in Early Colonial Peru.* Princeton: Princeton University Press.

_____. 1988. Atahualpa y el libro. *Revista de Indias* 48:693–714.

Mannheim, Bruce. 1991. *The Language of the Inka Since the European Invasion.* Austin: University of Texas Press.

March, Katherine. 1983. Weaving, Writing, and Gender. *Man* 18:729–744.

Masaquisa, Hugo. 1997. *Manual de Tinturación.* Quito: Abya Yala.

Masaquiza Masaquiza, José (Rumiñahui). 1995. Los Salasacas. In *Identidades indias en el Ecuador contemporáneo.* José Almeida Vinueza, ed. Pp. 213–246. Quito: Abya Yala.

Masiello, Francine. 1994. Literacy, Gender, and Transnational Meddling. In *Literacy: Interdisciplinary Conversations.* Deborah Keller-Cohen, ed. Pp. 229–248. Creskill, NJ: Hampton Press.

Mathur, Saloni. 2000. History and Anthropology in South Asia: Rethinking the Archive. *Annual Review of Anthropology* 29:89–106.

McEachern, C., and P. Mayer. 1986. The Children of Bronze and the Children of Gold: The Apolitical Anthropology of the Peasant. *Social Analysis* 19:70–77.

Meisch, Lynn. 1987. *Otavalo: Weaving, Costume and Market.* Quito: Ediciones Libri Mundi.

_____. 2002. *Andean Entrepreneurs: Merchants and Musicians in the Global Arena.* Austin: University of Texas Press.

_____, and Ann P. Rowe. 1998. Indigenous Ecuadorian Costume. In *Costume and Identity in Highland Ecuador.* Ann Pollard Rowe, ed. Pp. 39–49. Washington, DC: The Textile Museum.

Messick, Brinkley. 1989. Just Writing: Paradox and Political Economy in Yemeni Legal Documents. *Cultural Anthropology* 4:26–50.

_____. 1993. *The Calligraphic State: Textual Domination and History in a Muslim Society.* Berkeley: University of California Press.

Mignolo, Walter D. 1992. When Speaking Was Not Good Enough: Illiterates, Barbarians, Savages, and Cannibals. In *Amerindian Images and the Legacy of Columbus.* René Jara and Nicholas Spadaccini, eds. Pp. 312–345. Minneapolis: University of Minnesota Press.

_____. 1995. *The Darker Side of the Renaissance: Literacy, Territoriality, and Colonization.* Ann Arbor: University of Michigan Press.

Miller, Laura M. 1998. Tungurahua Province. In *Costume and Identity in Highland Ecuador.* Ann Pollard Rowe, ed. Pp. 126–144. Washington, DC: The Textile Museum.

Miller, Matthew. 2001. The Poor Man's Capitalist. *New York Times Magazine,* July 1:44–48.

Miner, Horace. 1956. Body Ritual among the Nacirema. *American Anthropologist* 58:503–507.

Moreno Yánez, Segundo E. 1983. La sociedad indígena y su articulación a la formación socioeconómica colonial en la Audiencia de Quito. In *Nueva historia del Ecuador: Epoca Colonial III.* Volume 5. Enrique Ayala Mora, ed. Pp. 96–136. Quito: Corporación Editora Nacional.

Morgan, Lynn M. 1998. Ambiguities Lost Fashioning the Fetus into a Child in Ecuador and the United States. In *Small Wars: The Cultural Politics of Childhood.* Nancy Scheper-Hughes, ed. Pp. 58–74. Berkeley: University of California Press.

Muratorio, Blanca. 1994. Introducción: Discursos y silencios sobre el indio en la conciencia nacional. In *Imágenes e imagineros: Representaciones de los indígenas ecuatorianos, siglos XIX y XX.* Blanca Muratorio, ed. Pp. 9–24. Quito: FLACSO.

Murra, John. 1962. Cloth and Its Function in the Inca State. *American Anthropologist* 64:710–728.

_____. 1980. *The Economic Organization of the Inka State.* Greenwich, CT: JAI Press.

Murray, David W. 1991. American/Indian. *Anthropology and Humanism Quarterly* 16:82–88.

Nicola, Gerardo. 1960. *La provincia de Tungurahua.* Ambato, Ecuador: Municipio de Ambato.

_____. 1987 [1960]. *La provincia de Tungurahua.* 2nd edition. Ambato, Ecuador: Municipio de Ambato.

_____. 1994 [1960] *La provincia de Tungurahua.* 3rd edition. Ambato, Ecuador: Municipio de Ambato.

Olson, David. 1994. *The World on Paper: The Conceptual and Cognitive Implications of Writing and Reading.* Cambridge: Cambridge University Press.

Orlove, Benjamin. 1991. Mapping Reeds and Reading Maps: The Politics of Representation in Lake Titicaca. *American Ethnologist* 18:3–38.

O'Rourke, Dennis. 1987. *Cannibal Tours.* Los Angeles: Direct Cinema Limited.

Ortiz Rescaniere, Alejandro. 1973. El mito de la escuela. In *Ideología mesiánica del mundo andino.* Juan M. Ossio, ed. Pp. 238–250. Lima: Ignacio Prado Pastor.

Ortner, Sherry. 1995. Resistance and the Problem of Ethnographic Refusal. *Comparative Studies in Society and History* 37:173–193.

Ossio, Juan M., ed. 1973. *Ideología mesiánica del mundo andino.* Lima: Ignacio Prado Pastor.

Parmentier, Richard. 1987. *The Sacred Remains: Myth, History, and Polity in Belau.* Chicago: University of Chicago Press.

_____. 1993. "The Semiotic Regimentation of Social Life." *Semiotica* 95:357–395.

Perrin, Michel. 1985. "Savage" Points of View on Writing. In *Myth and the Imaginary in the New World.* Edmundo Magaña and Peter Mason, eds. Pp. 211–231. Dordrecht, Netherlands: Centro de Estudios y Documentación Latinoamericanos.

Platt, Tristan. 1978. Identidad Andina y Conciencia Proletaria: Qhuyaruna y Ayllu en Norte de Potosí. *HISLA Revista Latinoamericana de Historia Económica y Social* (Lima) 2:47–73.

_____. 1992. Writing, Shamanism and Identity or Voices from Abya-Yala. *History Workshop Journal* 34:132–147.

Poeschel Rees, Ursula. 1985. *La mujer salasaca: Su situación en una época de reestructuración económico-cultural.* Quito: Abya Yala.

Poeschel-Renz, Ursula. 2001. *"No quisimos soltar el agua": formas de resistencia indígena y continuidad étnica en una comunidad ecuatoriana: 1960–1965.* Quito: Abya Yala.

Pollock, Donald K. 1993. Conversion and "Community" in Amazonia. In *Conversion to Christianity: Historical and Anthropological Perspectives on a Great Transformation*. Robert W. Hefner, ed. Pp. 165–197. Berkeley: University of California Press.

Prinsloo, Mastin, and Mignonne Breier, eds. 1996. *The Social Uses of Literacy: Theory and Practice in Contemporary South Africa*. Berthsam (South Africa): Sached Books; Philadelphia: John Benjamins.

Rama, Angel. 1984. *La ciudad letrada*. Hanover, NH: Ediciones del Norte.

Ramón Valarezo, Galo. 1991. Ese Secreto Poder de la Escritura. In *Una reflexión sobre el levantamiento indígena de 1990*. Ileana Almeida et al., eds. Pp. 351–371. Quito: Abya Yala.

Rappaport, Joanne. 1987. Mythic Images, Historical Thought and Printed Texts: The Páez and the Written Word. *Journal of Anthropological Research* 43:43–61.

_____. 1992. Fictive Foundations: National Romances and Subaltern Ethnicity in Latin America. *History Workshop Journal* 34:119–131.

_____. 1994a. *Cumbe Reborn: An Andean Ethnography of History*. Chicago: University of Chicago Press.

_____. 1994b. Legal Texts and Historical Interpretation: An Andean Ethnography of Reading. In *Exploring the Written: Anthropology and the Multiplicity of Writing*. Eduardo P. Archetti, ed. Pp. 277–296. Stockholm: Scandinavian University Press.

_____. 1994c. Object and Alphabet: Andean Indians and Documents in the Colonial Period. In *Writing Without Words: Alternative Literacies in Mesoamerica and the Andes*. Elizabeth Hill Boone and Walter D. Mignolo, eds. Pp. 271–291. Durham: Duke University Press.

_____. 1998 [1990]. *Politics of Memory: Native Historical Interpretations in the Colombian Andes*. 2nd edition. Durham: Duke University Press.

_____ and Thomas B. F. Cummins. 1994. Literacy and Power in Colonial Latin America. In *Social Construction of the Past: Representation as Power*. George C. Bond and Angela Gilliam, eds. Pp. 89–109. London: Routledge.

Rasnake, Roger. 1988a. *Domination and Cultural Resistance: Authority and Power Among an Andean People*. Durham: Duke University Press.

_____. 1988b. Images of Resistance to Colonial Domination. In *Rethinking History and Myth: Indigenous South American Perspectives on the Past*. Jonathan D. Hill, ed. Pp. 136–156. Urbana: University of Illinois Press.

Rivera Cusicanqui, Silvia. 1986. *Oprimidos pero no vencidos: Luchas del campesinado Aymara y Qhechwa de Bolivia, 1900–1980*. Geneva: Instituto de Investigaciones de las Naciones Unidas para el Desarrollo Social.

Rogers, Mark, ed. 1998. Performance, Identity and Historical Consciousness in the Andes. Theme Issue. *Journal of Latin American Anthropology* 3(2).

Roseberry, William. 1989. *Anthropologies and Histories*. New Brunswick: Rutgers University Press.

Rowe, C. J. 1988. *Plato: Phaedrus* (translation and commentary). Warminster, Wilts., England: Aris and Philips.

Rubio Orbe, Gonzalo. 1965. *Aspectos indígenas*. Quito: Casa de la Cultura.

Said, Edward. 1978. *Orientalism*. New York: Pantheon Books.

Salomon, Frank. 1981. Killing the Yumbo. In *Cultural Transformations and Ethnicity in Modern Ecuador*. Norman E. Whitten, Jr., ed. Pp. 162–208. Urbana: University of Illinois Press.

_____. 1986. *Native Lords of Quito in the Age of the Incas: The Political Economy of North Andean Chiefdoms*. Cambridge: Cambridge University Press.

_____, and Sue Grosboll. 1986. Names and Peoples in Incaic Quito: Retrieving Undocumented Historic Processes Through Anthroponymy and Statistics. *American Anthropologist* 88:387–399.

_____, and George L. Urioste. 1991. *The Huarochirí Manuscript: A Testament of Ancient and Colonial Andean Religion*. Austin: University of Texas Press.

Sánchez Parga, José. 1983. Estado y alfabetización. *Ecuador Debate* 2:59–71.

_____. 1989. *La observación, la memoria, y la palabra en la investigación social*. Quito: Centro Andino de Acción Popular.

Scollon, Ronald, and Susan Scollon. 1981. *Narrative, Literacy and Face in Interethnic Communication*. Norwood, NJ: Ablex.

Scott, James C. 1985. *Weapons of Resistance: Everyday Forms of Peasant Resistance*. New Haven: Yale University Press.

_____. 1990. *Domination and the Arts of Resistance: Hidden Transcripts*. New Haven: Yale University Press.

_____. 1998. *Seeing Like a State: How Certain Schemes to Improve the Human Condition Have Failed*. New Haven: Yale University Press.

Seed, Patricia. 1991. "Failing to Marvel": Atahualpa's Encounter with the Word. *American Research Review* 26:7–33.

Shryock, Andrew. 1997. *Nationalism and the Genealogical Imagination: Oral History and Textual Authority in Tribal Jordan*. Berkeley: University of California Press.

Silva, Armando. 1986. *Grafiti: Una ciudad imaginada*. Bogotá: Tercer Mundo Editores.

Silva, Erika. 1992. *Los mitos de la ecuatorianidad: Ensayo sobre la identidad nacional*. Quito: Abya Yala.

Silverblatt, Irene. 1987. *Moon, Sun, and Witches: Gender Ideologies and Class in Inca and Colonial Peru*. Princeton: Princeton University Press.

_____. 1995. Becoming Indian in the Central Andes of Seventeenth Century Peru. In *After Colonialism: Imperial Histories and Postcolonial Displacements*. Gyan Prakash, ed. Pp. 279–298. Princeton: Princeton University Press.

Silverstein, Michael. 1979. Language Structure and Linguistic Ideology. In *The Elements: A Parasession on Linguistic Units and Levels*. Paul R. Clyne, William F. Hanks, and Carol L. Hofbauer, eds. Pp. 193–247. Chicago: Chicago Linguistic Society.

_____. 1999. Whorfianism and the Linguistic Imagination of Nationality. In *Regimes of Language: Ideologies, Polities, and Identities*. Paul V. Kroskrity, ed. Pp. 85–138. Santa Fe, NM: School of American Research.

Skar, Sarah Lund. 1994. On the Margin: Letter Exchange among Andean Non-Literates. In *Exploring the Written: Anthropology and the Multiplicity of Writing*. Eduardo P. Archetti, ed. Pp. 261–276. Stockholm: Scandinavian University Press.

Smith, Richard Saumarez. 1996. *Rule by Records: Land Registration and Village Custom in Early British Punjab*. Delhi: Oxford University Press.

Stark, Louisa R. 1981. Folk Models of Stratification and Ethnicity in the Highlands of Northern Ecuador. In *Cultural Transformations and Ethnicity in Modern Ecuador*. Norman E. Whitten, Jr., ed. Pp. 387–401. Urbana: University of Illinois Press.

———. 1985a. Ecuadorian Highland Quichua: History and Current Status. In *South American Indian Languages: Retrospect and Prospect*. Harriet E. Manelis and Louisa R. Stark, eds. Pp. 445–479. Austin: University of Texas Press.

———. 1985b. The Role of Women in Peasant Uprisings in the Ecuadorian Highlands. In *Political Anthropology in Ecuador: Perspectives from Indigenous Cultures*. Jeffrey Ehrenreich, ed. Pp. 3–24. Albany, NY: Society for Latin American Anthropology.

Stark, Louisa R., and Pieter C. Muysken. 1977. *Diccionario Español-Quichua, Quichua-Español*. Publicaciones de los Museos del Banco Central del Ecuador, No. 1. Guayaquil, Ecuador: Museo del Banco Central.

Starn, Orin. 1999. *Nightwatch: The Politics of Protest in the Andes*. Durham, NC: Duke University Press.

Street, Brian. 1984. *Literacy in Theory and Practice*. Cambridge: Cambridge University Press.

———. 1987. Orality and Literacy as Ideological Constructions: Some Problems in Cross-Cultural Studies. *Culture and History* 2:7–30.

———. 1995. *Social Literacies: Critical Perspectives on Literacy in Development, Ethnography and Education*. London: Longman.

———. 1999. "The Meanings of Literacy." In *Literacy: An International Handbook*. Daniel Wagner, Richard L. Venezky, and Brian V. Street, eds. Pp. 34–40. Boulder: Westview Press.

———, ed. 1993. *Cross-Cultural Approaches to Literacy*. Cambridge: Cambridge University Press.

Stutzman, Ronald. 1981. *El Mestizaje*: An All-Inclusive Ideology of Exclusion. In *Cultural Transformations and Ethnicity in Modern Ecuador*. Norman E. Whitten, Jr., ed. Pp. 45–94. Urbana: University of Illinois Press.

Sutton, David E. 1991. Is Anybody Out There? Anthropology and the Question of Audience. *Critique of Anthropology* 11:91–104.

———. 1994. "Tradition and Modernity": Kalymnian Constructions of Identity and Otherness. *Journal of Modern Greek Studies* 12:239–260.

———. 1998. *Memories Cast in Stone: The Relevance of the Past in Everyday Life*. New York: Berg.

———. 2001. *Remembrance of Repasts: An Anthropology of Food and Memory*. New York: Berg.

Taussig, Michael. 1980. *The Devil and Commodity Fetishism in South America*. Chapel Hill: University of North Carolina Press.

———. 1987. *Shamanism, Colonialism, and the Wild Man: A Study in Terror and Healing*. Chicago: University of Chicago Press.

_____. 1998. Viscerality, Faith, and Skepticism: Another Theory of Magic. In *Near Ruins: Cultural Theory at the End of the Century*. Nicholas Dirks, ed. Pp. 221–256. Minneapolis: University of Minnesota Press.

Tedlock, Barbara, and Dennis Tedlock. 1985. Text and Textile: Language and Technology in the Art of the Quiché Maya. *Journal of Anthropological Research* 41:121–147.

Terán, Francisco. 1972. *Geografía del Ecuador*. Quito: Gráfica CYMA.

Thompson, Paul. 1988 [1978]. *The Voice of the Past: Oral History*. 2nd edition. Oxford: Oxford University Press.

Tilley, Christopher. 1997. Performing Culture in the Global Village. *Critique of Anthropology* 17:67–89.

Todorov, Tzvetan. 1984. *The Conquest of America*. Richard Howard, trans. New York: Harper and Row.

Tolen, Rebecca Jane. 1995. Wool and Synthetics, Countryside and City: Dress, Race and History in Chimborazo, Highland Ecuador. Ph.D. dissertation, Anthropology Department, University of Chicago.

Trouillot, Michel-Rolph. 1986. The Price of Indulgence. *Social Analysis* 19:85–90.

Turner, Terence. 1986. Production, Exploitation and Social Consciousness in the "Peripheral Situation." *Social Analysis* 19:91–116.

_____. 1988. Ethno-Ethnohistory: Myth and History in Native South American Representations of Contact with Western Society. In *Rethinking History and Myth: Indigenous South American Perspectives on the Past*. Jonathan D. Hill, ed. Pp. 235–281. Urbana: University of Illinois Press.

_____. 1991. Representing, Resisting, Rethinking: Historical Transformations of Kayapo Culture and Anthropological Consciousness. In *Colonial Situations: Essays on the Contextualization of Ethnographic Knowledge*. George W. Stocking, Jr., ed. Pp. 285–313. Madison: University of Wisconsin Press.

Urban, Greg, and Joel Sherzer, eds. 1991. *Nation-States and Indians in Latin America*. Austin: University of Texas Press.

Urla, Jacqueline. 1993. Cultural Politics in an Age of Statistics: Numbers, Nations, and the Making of Basque Identity. *American Ethnologist* 20:818–843.

Volinsky, Nan Leigh. 1998. Violin Performance, Practice, and Ethnicity in Saraguro, Ecuador. Ph.D. dissertation, Anthropology Department, University of Illinois at Urbana-Champaign.

Wachtel, Nathan. 1973. La visión de los vencidos: La conquista española en el folklore indígena. In *Ideología mesiánica del mundo andino*. Juan M. Ossio, ed. Pp. 37–81. Lima: Ignacio Prado Pastor.

Wade, Peter. 1997. *Race and Ethnicity in Latin America*. London: Pluto Press.

_____. 1994. *Gods and Vampires: Return to Chipaya*. Chicago: University of Chicago Press.

Wagner, Daniel A. 1993. *Literacy, Culture, and Development: Becoming Literate in Morocco*. Cambridge: Cambridge University Press.

Warren, Kay B. 1989 [1978]. *The Symbolism of Subordination: Indian Identity in a Guatemalan Town*. 2nd edition. Austin: University of Texas Press.

Waskosky, Kristine E. 1992. Affixes of Salasaca Quichua with Special Attention to Derivational Affixes Which Attach to Verbs. Master's Thesis, Department of Linguistics, University of North Dakota.

Waskosky, S. Peter. 1992. *La Fonología del Quichua de Salasaca*. Ambato, Ecuador: Casa de Montalvo.

Weismantel, Mary. 1988. *Food, Gender, and Poverty in the Ecuadorian Andes*. Philadelphia: University of Pennsylvania Press.

_____. 1991. Maize Beer and Andean Social Transformations: Drunken Indians, Bread Babies, and Chosen Women. *MLN* 106:861–879.

_____. 2001. *Cholas and Pishtacos: Stories of Race and Sex in the Andes*. Chicago: University of Chicago Press.

Weiss, Wendy A. 1993. "Gringo . . . Gringita." *Anthropological Quarterly* 66:187–196.

Whitten, Norman E., Jr. 1981. Introduction. In *Cultural Transformations and Ethnicity in Modern Ecuador*. Norman E. Whitten, Jr., ed. Pp. 1–44. Urbana: University of Illinois Press.

_____. 1986 [1974]. *Black Frontiersmen: A South American Case*. 2nd edition. Prospect Heights, Illinois: Waveland Press.

_____. 1988. Historical and Mythic Evocations of Chthonic Power in South America. In *Rethinking History and Myth: Indigenous South American Perspectives on the Past*. Jonathan D. Hill, ed. Pp. 282–306. Urbana: University of Illinois Press.

_____. 1996. The Ecuadorian Levatamiento Indígena of 1990 and the Epitomizing Symbol of 1992: Reflections on Nationalism, Ethnic-Bloc Formation, and Racialist Ideologies. In *History, Power, Identity: Ethnogenesis in the Americas, 1492–1992*. Jonathan D. Hill, ed. Pp. 193–217. Iowa City: University of Iowa Press.

Wogan, Peter. 1994. Perceptions of European Literacy in Early Contact Situations. *Ethnohistory* 41:407–429.

_____. 2001. Imagined Communities Reconsidered: Is Print-Capitalism What We Think It Is? *Anthropological Theory* 1:403–418.

Wongpaithoon, Jiraporn. 1996. Thailand Residents Look for Good Luck in Monk. *The Sun Herald* (Biloxi, MS), November 26: A6.

Woolard, Kathryn A., and Bambi B. Schieffelin. 1994. Language Ideology. *Annual Review of Anthropology* 23: 55–82.

Zuidema, R. Tom. 1977. The Inca Kinship System: A New Theoretical View. In *Andean Kinship and Marriage*. Ralph Bolton and Enrique Mayer, eds. Pp. 240–281. Washington, DC: American Anthropological Association.

Zurita Herrera, Guadencio. 1992. *1990: El Censo*. Quito: Instituto Nacional de Estadística y Censos.

Index